Carolyn Lanchner

Roy Lichtenstein

The Museum of Modern Art, New York

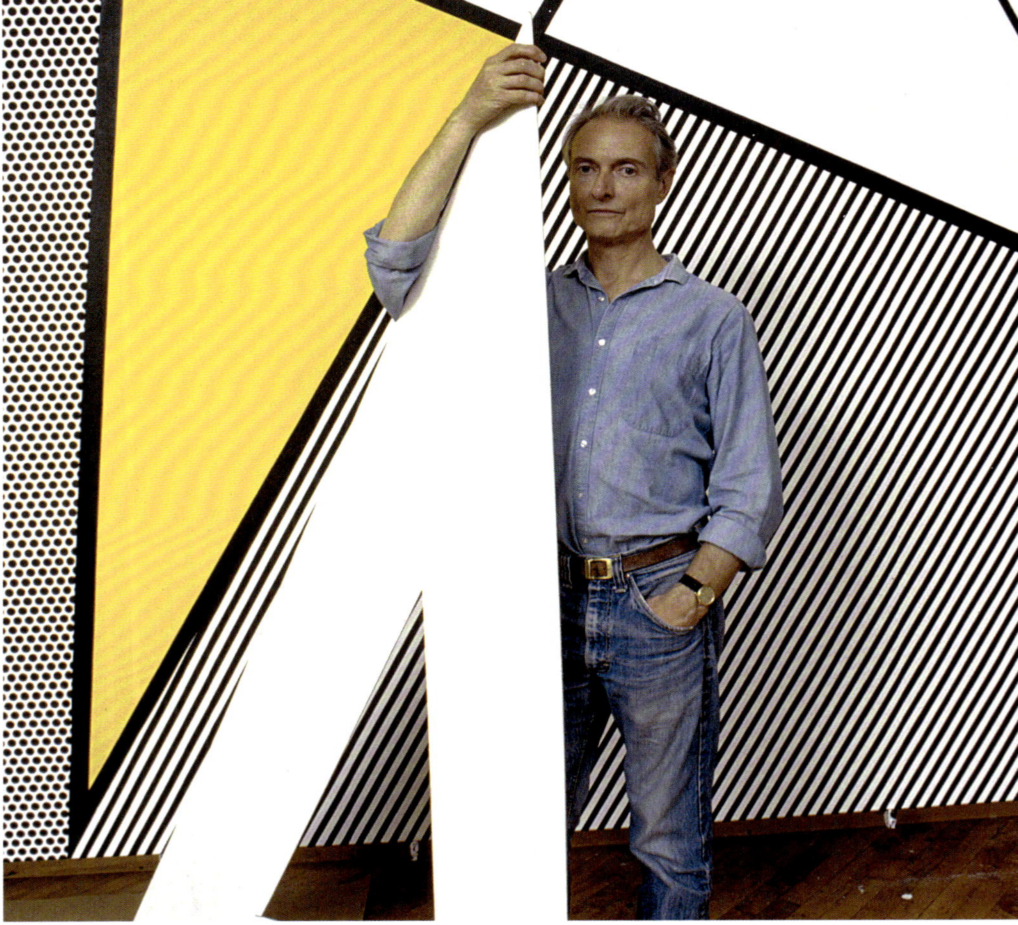

Roy Lichtenstein with *Perfect Painting #1*
in his New York studio, 1985

This book presents ten works selected from the more than 180 pieces by Roy Lichtenstein in the collection of The Museum of Modern Art. The first work by Lichtenstein to enter the Museum's collection, in 1964, was a contribution by the artist to the illustrated book *1 Cent Life* made the same year; it was followed by prints, drawings, paintings, and sculptures, including *Modern Painting with Bolt* (discussed here on p. 17) in 1967 and *Drowning Girl* (p. 11) in 1971. Lichtenstein's painting *Girl with Ball* (p. 5), acquired in 1981, is a highlight of the Museum's collection. Lichtenstein's works were included in a dozen group shows at the Museum between 1965 and 1987, and in 1987 MoMA mounted the first comprehensive retrospective of Lichtenstein's drawings; it was the first show of drawings by a living artist presented at the Museum. In the accompanying catalogue, curator Bernice Rose describes Lichtenstein as "a consummately skillful artist. . . . At once eager, discerning, and tough." This book is one in a series featuring artists represented in depth in the Museum's collection.

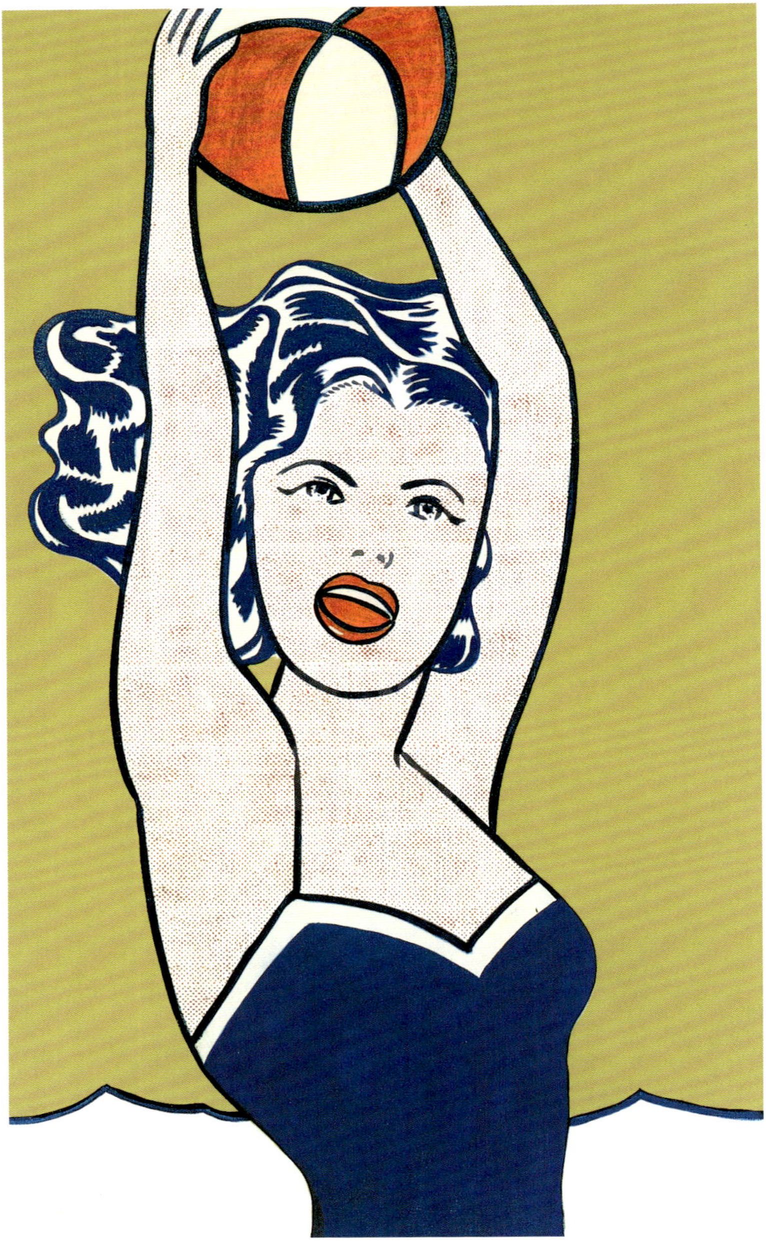

Girl with Ball 1961
Oil and synthetic polymer paint on canvas,
60 1/4 x 36 1/4" (153 x 91.9 cm)
The Museum of Modern Art, New York.
Gift of Philip Johnson, 1981

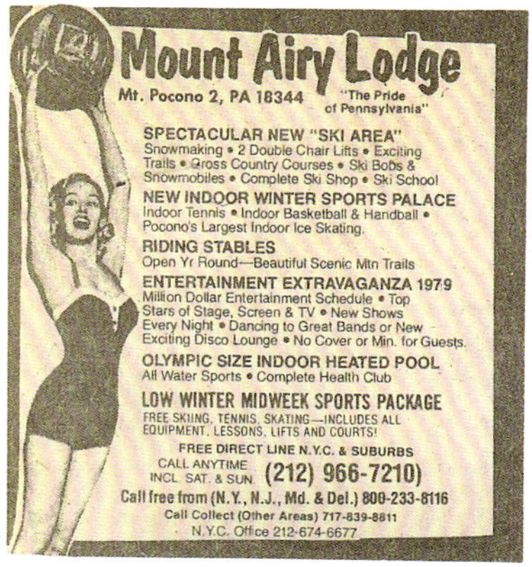

Girl with Ball (1961)

This image of a blandly seductive young woman is a riff on the charms of an earthier beauty touting the pleasures of Mount Airy Lodge, "The Pride of Pennsylvania," in an advertisement that ran for over two decades in newspapers in the New York area (fig. 1). The appearance and pictorial genealogy of Lichtenstein's figure affronted an art world still loyal to the gestural freedom and romantic spirit of Abstract Expressionism. Where in the past Lichtenstein had sometimes applied the sophistication of accepted, often Picasso-like styles to the depiction of what an artist friend called "corny" subject matter (figs. 2 and 3), in 1961 he definitively made the move to a practice that consistently used cultural clichés to challenge the aesthetic clichés of high art. Comic strips, advertisements, and selected objects from the consumer marketplace served as contemporary counterparts to Marcel Duchamp's urinal and bicycle wheel; they were, the artist said, "'ready-made' ways of doing everything I wanted to do."

Many in Lichtenstein's audience of the early 1960s considered the subjects of his paintings to have been no more tampered with than Duchamp's store-bought objects—images lifted almost

1 Advertisement for Mount Airy Lodge, Poconos, Pennsylvania, in the travel section of the *New York Times*, 1963

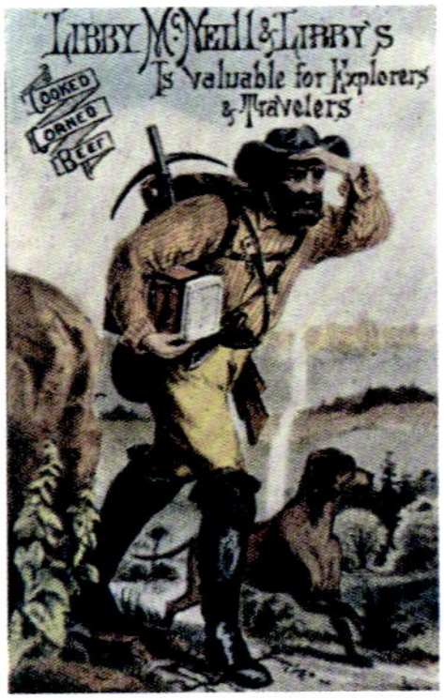

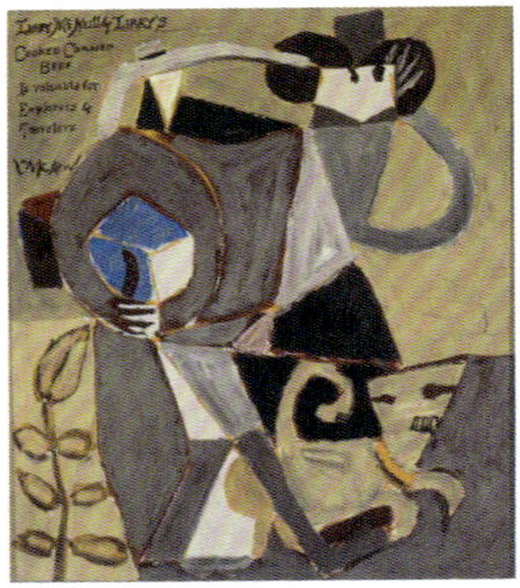

intact from their commercial sources. It was a reaction the artist was looking for: "The closer my work is to the original, the more threatening and critical the content." But, he added, "I think my paintings are critically transformed." *Girl with Ball*'s deviations from its ready-made inspiration amply bear out Lichtenstein's assessment. On the most obvious level, a shift in scale from a one-column newspaper advertisement to a life-size image, combined with a transition from black-and-white printed reproduction on newspaper stock to Mondrian-like harmonies of red, yellow, and blue on canvas, necessarily produces an intensity of mood beyond the reach or ambition of its source. Aside from these elemental changes, the artist manipulated the girl's figure to endow the painting with something of the visual impact of hard-edge abstract painting. To paraphrase Lichtenstein, he was at the time aiming at "anti-Cubist" composition, defined by him as the isolation of an "object on a blank ground," thus defying "the major direction of art since the early Renaissance, which has more and more symbolized the integration of 'figure' with 'ground.'"

Passing from the arena of life into the hermetic space of art, Mount Airy's pinup girl trades lusty vitality and its diffuse associations for an exquisitely calibrated unity. Her figure, abbreviated to

2 Advertisement for Libby, McNeill, & Libby's Cooked Corned Beef, reproduced in *Life* magazine, July 4, 1949

3 *The Explorer* c. 1952
Oil on canvas, 16 x 14" (40.7 x 35.6 cm)
The Butler Institute of American Art, Youngstown, Ohio. Gift of Mr. and Mrs. Robert Miller, 1960

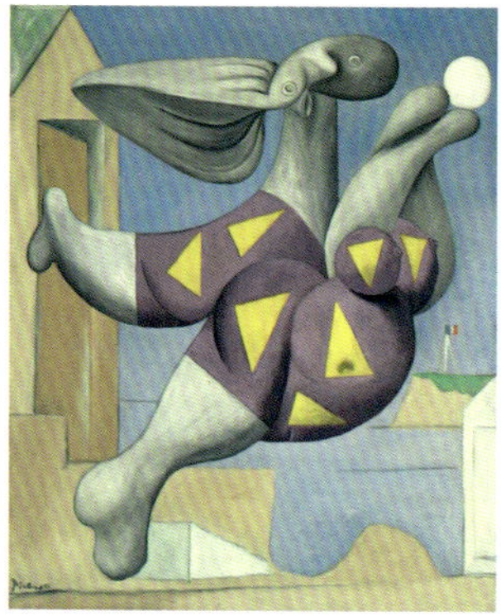

half-length, is no longer an agglomeration of robust parts but is joined by pictorial rhyme and defined by a single, uninterrupted line. Her bathing suit's white, heart-shaped neckline is repeated and inversed in her red-and-white amphibian mouth, again in the part of her hair, and once more with variations in the red-and-white ball at the top of the picture. At the bottom, the blue-edged water takes part in the game. Her origins on the printed page are alluded to in the simulated benday dots of her flesh—literally and visually they form a screen, equating her presence with the planarity of the canvas support.

Like all art, this girl with a ball is artifice; she also falls into the category termed representational. But she is not realist, not a copy of life, but a copy of a copy. As one of Lichtenstein's most reproduced and by now most familiar images, *Girl with Ball* has achieved an individual fame roughly on a par with Pablo Picasso's *Bather with Beach Ball* of 1932 (fig. 4), an extravagantly improbable "unreal" image that nonetheless gives form to the all-consuming reality of the artist's obsession with his young mistress. Far from an expression of organic involvement with her creator, Lichtenstein's bather is the dispassionate evidence of his passionate commitment to style.

4 Pablo Picasso (Spanish, 1881–1973)
Bather with Beach Ball 1932
Oil on canvas, 57 $^7/_8$ x 45 $^1/_8$" (146.2 x 114.6 cm)
The Museum of Modern Art, New York. Partial gift of an anonymous donor and promised gift of Jo Carole and Ronald S. Lauder, 1980

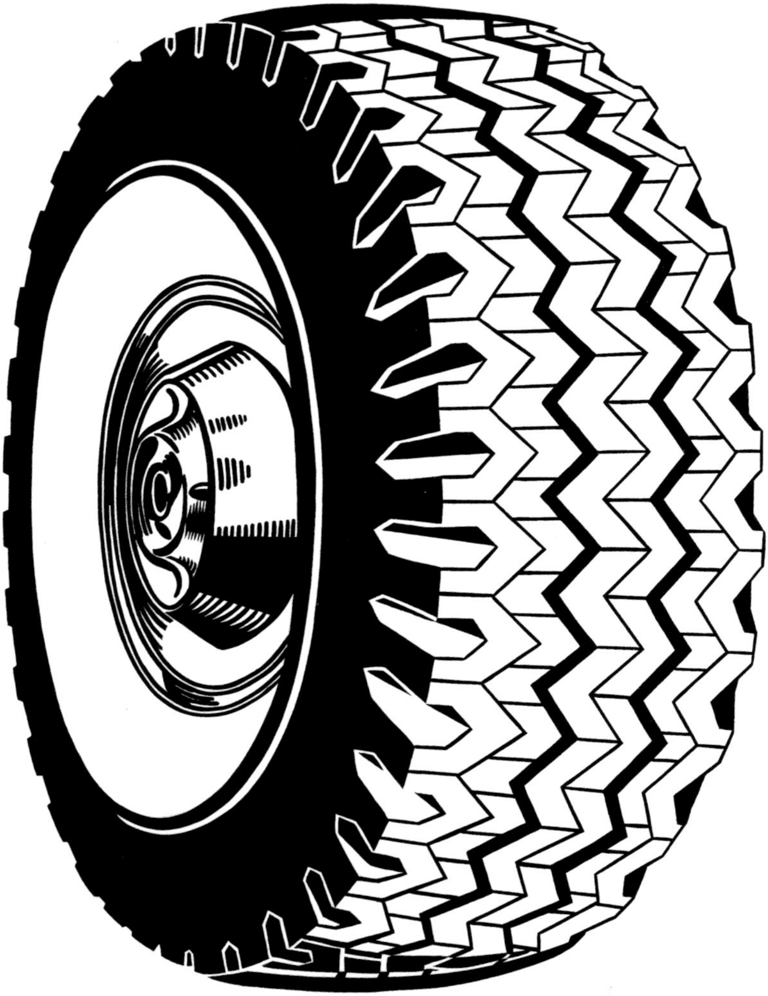

Tire 1962
Oil on canvas, 68 x 58" (172.7 x 147.3 cm)
The Museum of Modern Art, New York.
Fractional gift of Mr. and Mrs. Donald G.
Fisher in honor of Kirk Varnedoe, 2001

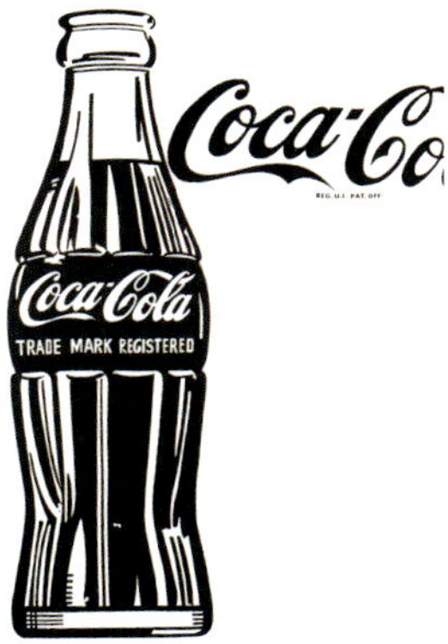

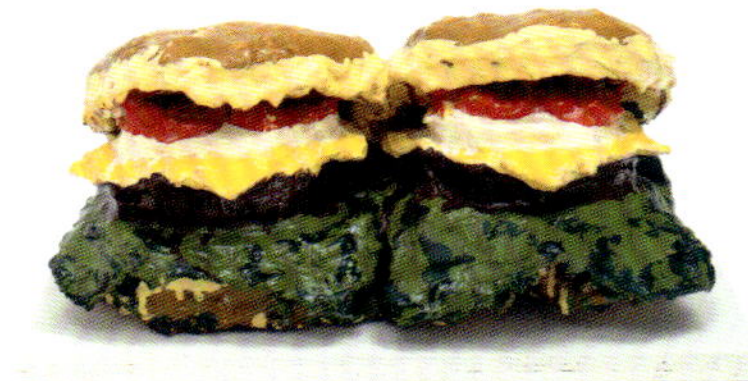

Tire (1962) When Lichtenstein made this still-astonishing life-size picture of a tire, he was not alone in irreverently stretching the time-honored conventions of still-life painting. Andy Warhol was making *Large Coca-Cola* (fig. 5), Jim Dine had already concentrated on a shoe, and Claes Oldenburg was interested in foodstuffs (fig. 6), to name only a few of the young artists then grouped by largely puzzled, sometimes disgruntled critics under such formulations as neo-Dada, New Sign Painting, and New American Dream. By the next year, when the term Pop art had definitively taken hold, these artists, who had developed their individual manners in relative isolation, were well aware of each other and their shared preference for subjects drawn from American consumer culture. Beyond that and their new group identity, their styles were as distinctive as their personalities.

There were, however, brief moments when works by Lichtenstein and Warhol seemed to intersect. Both liked to profile dumb, subaesthetic objects in black paint against stark uninflected grounds, as Lichtenstein did in *Tire* and Warhol in *Large Coca-Cola*. There is, however, a crucial difference between them.

5 Andy Warhol (American, 1928–1987)
Coca-Cola (Large Coca-Cola) 1962
Acrylic, pencil, and Letraset on linen, 6' 9 5/8" x 56 7/8" (207.3 x 144.5 cm)
Collection Elisabeth and Michael Rea

6 Claes Oldenburg (American, born Sweden 1929)
Two Cheeseburgers, with Everything (Dual Hamburgers) 1962
Burlap soaked in plaster, painted with enamel, 7 x 14 3/4 x 8 5/8" (17.8 x 37.5 x 21.8 cm)
The Museum of Modern Art, New York. Philip Johnson Fund, 1962

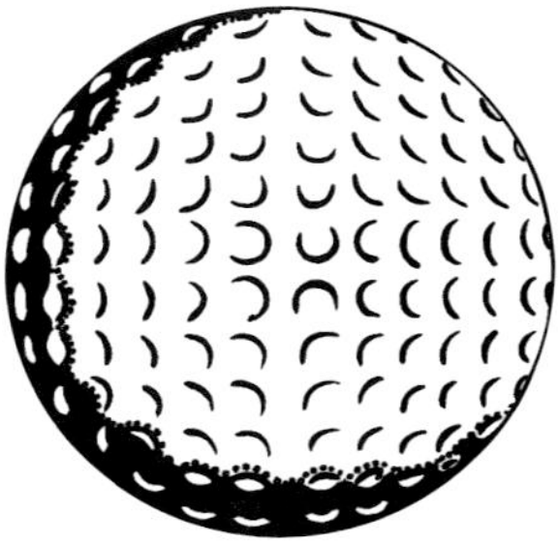

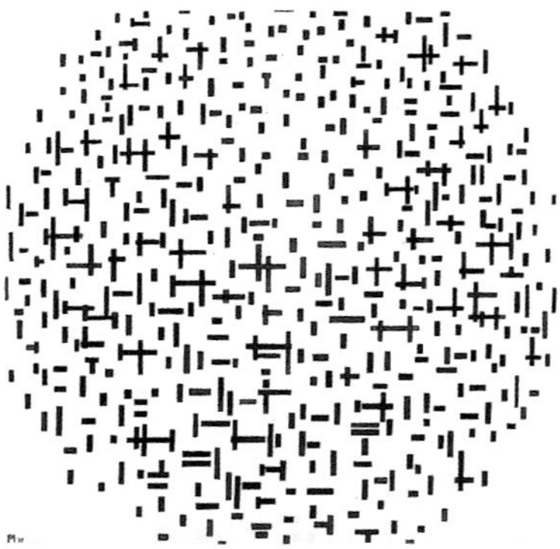

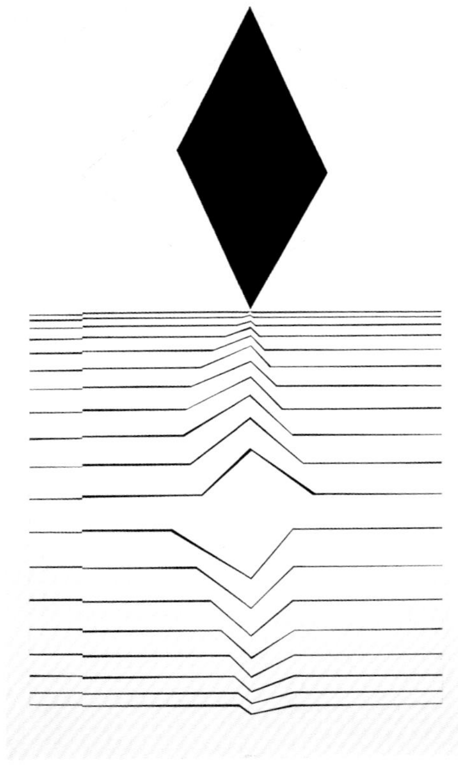

Top:
7 *Golf Ball* 1962
Oil on canvas, 32 x 32" (81.3 x 81.3 cm)
Private collection

8 Piet Mondrian (Dutch, 1872–1944)
Composition in Line 1916–17
Oil on canvas, 42 1/2 x 42 1/2" (108 x 108 cm)
Kröller-Müller Museum, Otterlo, the Netherlands. © 2009 Mondrian/Holtzman Trust c/o HCR International, Warrentown, Va.

9 Victor Vasarely (French, 1908–1997)
Mizzar 1956–60
Oil on canvas in painted wood frame, 6' 5" x 46 1/8" x 1 5/8" (197.7 x 117.2 x 4.2 cm)
Hirshhorn Museum and Sculpture Garden, Smithsonian Institution, Washington, D.C.
Gift of Joseph H. Hirshhorn, 1972

Where Lichtenstein's object is generic, a platonic ideal of a tire, Warhol's is specific, a branded bottle that is an icon of Americanness. Free of temporal limitations, the tire's banal anonymity allows it to occupy its ground with an implacable if slightly wacky *there*ness.

Unmistakably readable as a three-quarter view of the wheel of an automobile with hubcap and tire tread, the painting's meticulous rendering calls attention to its subject's abstract qualities. Just as Lichtenstein played with the Mondrian-like qualities of a golf ball in another painting of 1962 (figs. 7 and 8), in this work he was no doubt amused to point out reverberations of Victor Vasarely's "scientific" abstract art (fig. 9) in the architectural patterns of a tire tread. With broader intent, Lichtenstein's *Tire* and *Golf Ball* and his other black-and-white still lifes of the early 1960s constitute both an affable salute and a rejoinder to the heroic black-and-white Abstract Expressionist paintings by the likes of Franz Kline, Robert Motherwell, Barnett Newman, Willem de Kooning, and Jackson Pollock.

Drowning Girl (1963) Nearly submerged, this lovely young woman is in the very process of consigning herself to the watery depths. That her plight seems more bemusing than affecting has, of course, to do with her instantly obvious origins in a comic strip. Interviewed the year he painted this unhappy girl, Lichtenstein discussed his "complete break" in the summer of 1961 with his Abstract Expressionist style of the

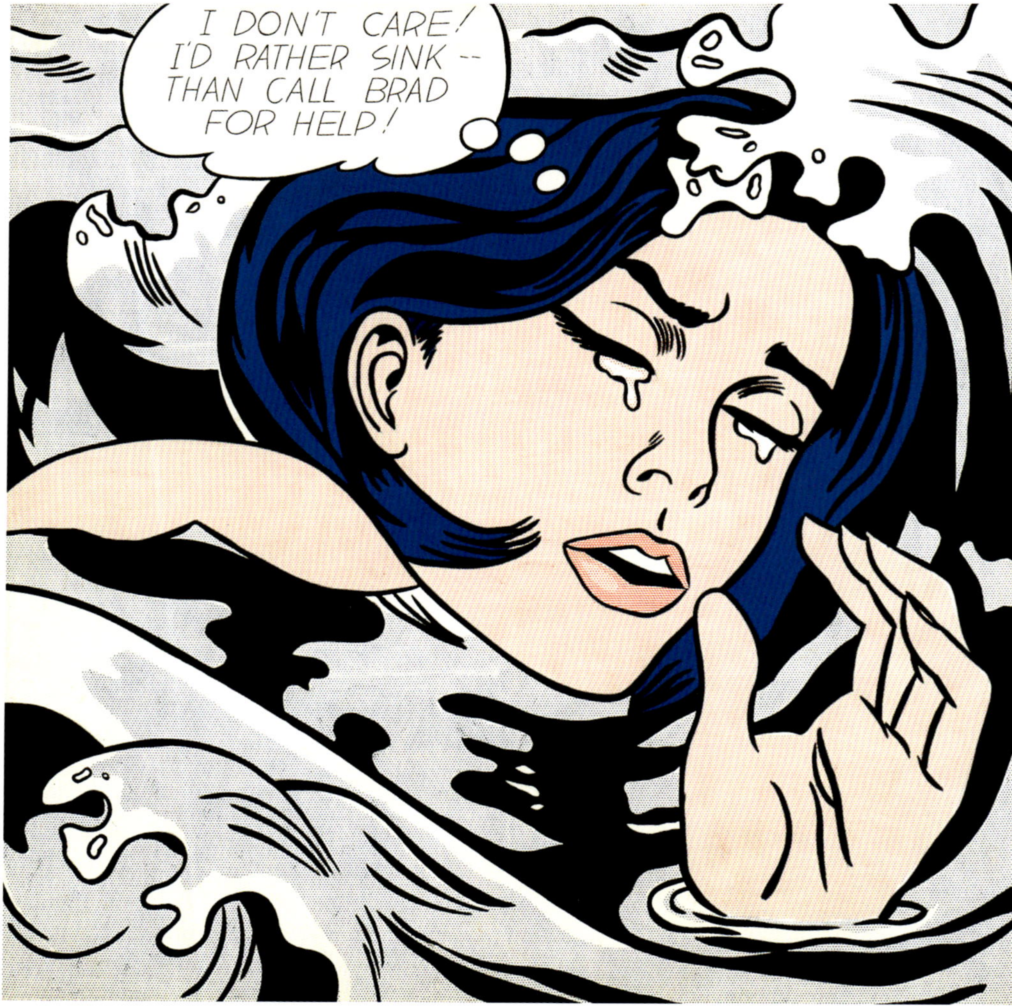

Drowning Girl 1963
Oil and synthetic polymer paint on canvas,
67 5/8 x 66 3/4" (171.6 x 169.5 cm)
The Museum of Modern Art, New York.
Philip Johnson Fund (by exchange) and gift
of Mr. and Mrs. Bagley Wright, 1971

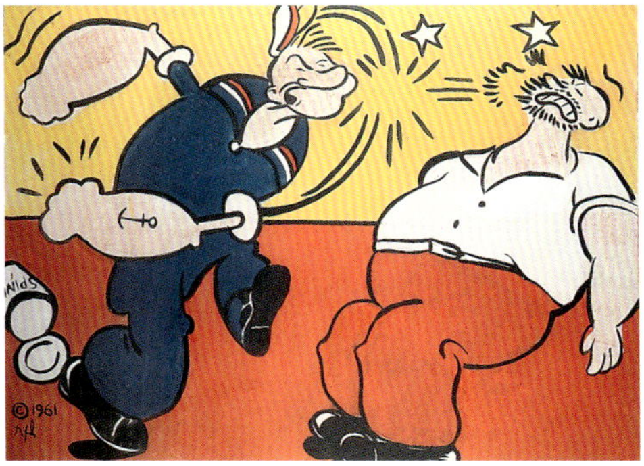

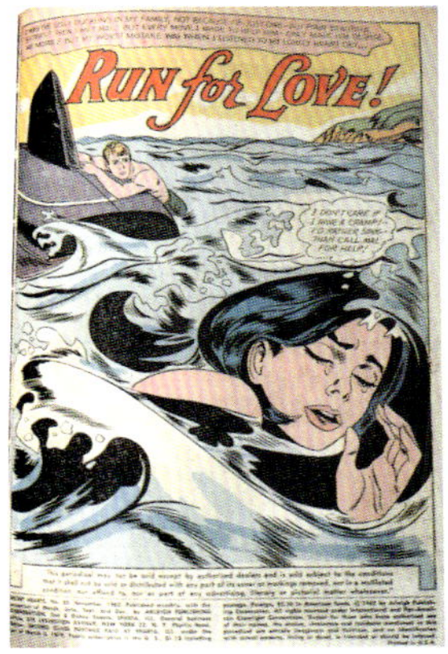

previous four years in favor of cartoon imagery. "The early ones were of animated cartoons, Donald Duck, Mickey Mouse, and Popeye [fig. 10], but then I shifted into the style of cartoon books with a more serious content such as 'Armed Forces at War' and 'Teen Romance.' . . . I was very excited about, and interested in, the highly emotional content yet detached impersonal handling of love, hate, war, etc., in these cartoon images."

In *Drowning Girl*, derived from the 1962 DC Comics book *Secret Hearts* (fig. 11), the contrast between highly charged content and cool handling has been not only preserved but intensified. Translating the cartoon to art, Lichtenstein used a process he characterized thus: "As directly as possible. . . . From a cartoon, photograph or whatever, I draw a small picture—the size that will fit into my opaque projector. . . . I don't draw a picture in order to reproduce it—I do it in order to recompose it. . . . I project the drawing onto the canvas and pencil it in and then I play around with the drawing until it satisfies me."

Lichtenstein's early "playing around" with *Drowning Girl*'s drawing apparently led to a fairly radical recomposition of the source image. Tightening its focus, the artist discarded its

10 *Popeye* 1961
Oil on canvas, 42 x 56" (106.7 x 142.2 cm)
Private collection

11 Tony Abruzzo. Panel from "Run for Love!" in *Secret Hearts*, no. 83 (November 1962). DC Comics

vertical shape and the distracting imagery of overturned boat, befuddled boyfriend, and distant seascape to concentrate on an equable balance of the girl's head within a not-quite-perfect square. This new format provided Lichtenstein with the ideal field to impose a governing unity on his source material, to make, as he said, the "brittle images" of the comic strip "yield to compositional purposes." Through a series of variously evident maneuvers the artist used the hospitable space of the square to assist in the creation of an enveloping vortical movement. Its swirling career around the canvas is carried by a newly energized white wave swooping down and into the picture from the left in a dipping curve, momentarily offering the girl pictorial buoyancy before curling in an upward thrust that circles her face and breaks over her head in strangely animate white foam. To accommodate this aquatic continuum, Lichtenstein moved the thought balloon to the upper left, where it is visually no more dissonant than any other bubble that might be afloat on the leftward current of the subsiding wave.

Further enhancing the fluidity and animation of the composition is Lichtenstein's admirably enterprising use of black. By and large it shows up where it does in the source image, but in the area below the girl's chin, for example, it appears to have been endowed with unexpected abilities. In inky, lantern-slide silhouette, the girl's hand and her indented shoulder are reflected against the pale-blue benday-dot water as two fierce combatants straight out of Disneyland. Not dissimilar but less explicit allusions attach to the three breaking waves described in black at the picture's corners. But black is also implicated in

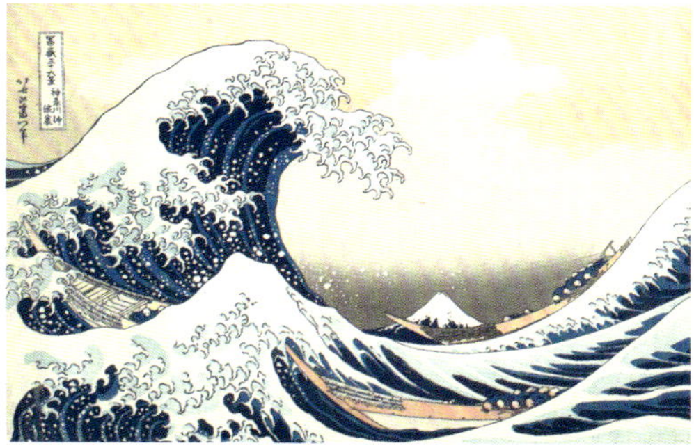

other, more high-art associations. Many critics have seen the swirling blacks in the girl's blue hair as deliberate references to the airborne arabesques of Jackson Pollock's classic poured paintings. And no one has disagreed with Lichtenstein, who said, "In the *Drowning Girl*, the water is not only Art Nouveau, but it can also be seen as Hokusai [fig. 12]. I saw it and then pushed it a little further until it was a reference most people will get. I don't think it is terribly significant, but it is a way of crystallizing the style by exaggeration."

Before leaving this girl in her forever precarious position, we might note that Lichtenstein edited not only the image but the text in the balloon as well. Cutting out "I have a cramp," he left his doughty heroine with the more universal statement "I don't care." In addition, he felt this stereotype of American womanhood deserved a boyfriend with "a heroic name"—hence the idiosyncratic Mal became Brad. It was, the artist said, "a very minor idea, but it has to do with oversimplification and cliché," both of which Lichtenstein exploited in the most complex and unexpected manner.

12 Katsushika Hokusai (Japanese, 1760–1849)
The Great Wave at Kanagawa (from a Series of Thirty-Six Views of Mount Fuji) c. 1830–32
Polychrome woodblock print, 10 1/8 x 14 15/16"
(25.7 x 37.9 cm)
The Metropolitan Museum of Art, H. O. Havemeyer Collection. Bequest of Mrs. H. O. Havemeyer, 1929

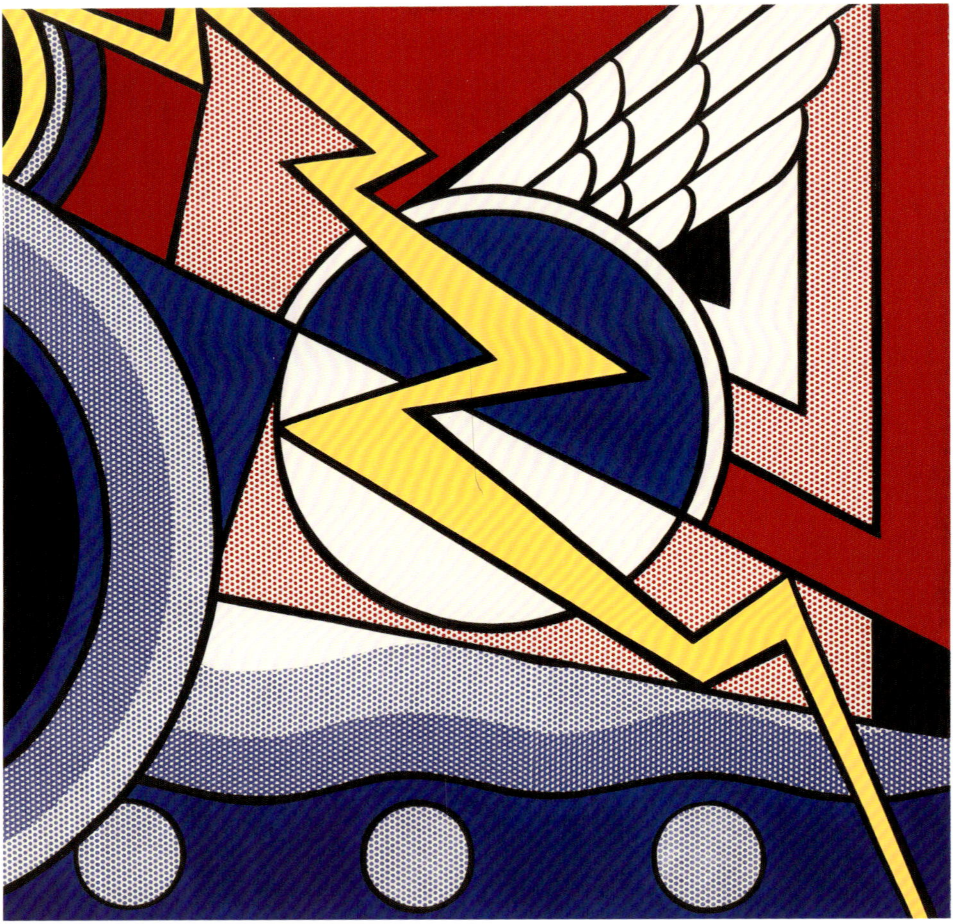

Modern Painting with Bolt 1966
Synthetic polymer paint and oil partly screenprinted on canvas, 68 1/4 x 68 3/8"
(173.2 x 173.5 cm)
The Museum of Modern Art, New York.
The Sidney and Harriet Janis Collection, 1967

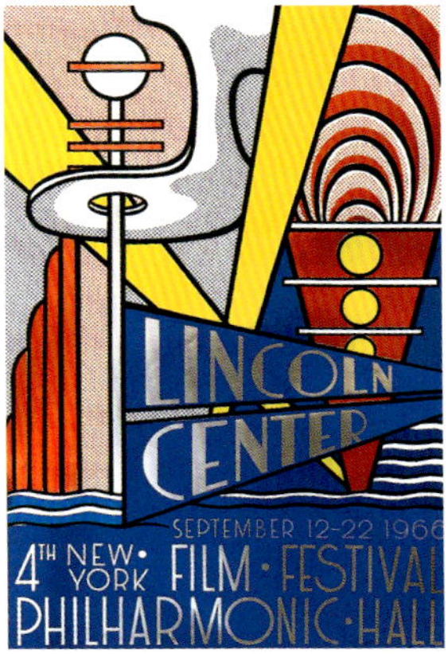

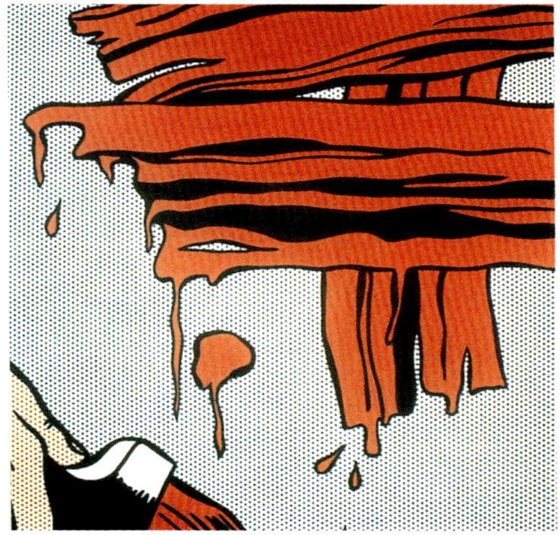

Modern Painting with Bolt

(1966) This is one of the most structurally compact of the paintings in the Modern series Lichtenstein began with a poster for Lincoln Center in the summer of 1966 (fig. 13). Like all the other work in the group it is stylistically unmistakable as a spin-off from 1920s and 1930s Art Deco architecture and design and is less paraphrase than synthesis. With the exception of his slightly earlier Brushstroke paintings (fig. 14), almost all of Lichtenstein's previous work depends on a preconceived format: an advertisement, a cartoon, or, in the single-image paintings, an object of basically invariant shape, such as a tire or golf ball—all things that are part of our common cultural experience. Equally prevalent in mid-twentieth-century life—at least to the many who noticed—were Abstract Expressionism's highly publicized gestural extravagances and Art Deco's ubiquitous presence in wallpaper, furniture, and such public buildings as New York's Radio City Music Hall. In undertaking his Brushstroke and Modern series Lichtenstein was no longer focusing on a discrete entity

13 *Lincoln Center Poster* 1966
Screenprint, 45 13/16 x 30" (116.4 x 76.2 cm)
Lincoln Center/List Art Posters, New York

14 *Brushstrokes* 1965
Oil and Magna on canvas, 48 x 48"
(121.9 x 121.9 cm)
Private collection

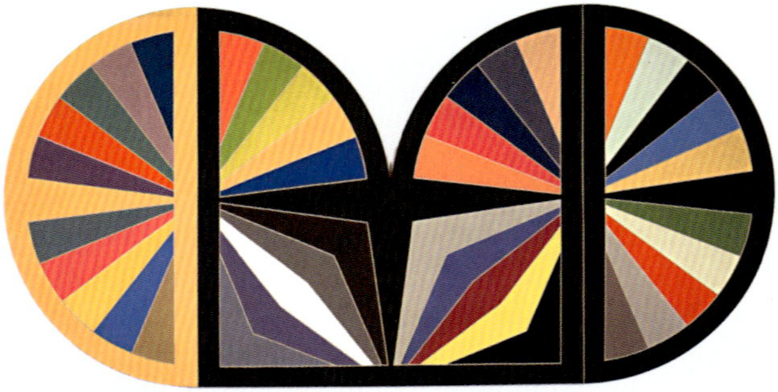

but codifying a style: in the earlier group through a focus on its single most salient characteristic, and in the later through precisely balanced phrases from a grand, if limited, historical vocabulary.

In *Modern Painting with Bolt* Lichtenstein gave a succinct, two-part title to a complex painting devised with deliberate economy—his palette restricted to his usual Mondrian-like primaries and his figuration to the chosen idiom of Art Deco. Where later, larger pictures in the series depend on strategically employed diagonals to organize a diffuse lateral expanse, in this composition a single bolt of yellow lightning slashing diagonally across a square compact field dominates all other pictorial action. Its jagged entry into a field of harmoniously interlocking geometries carries a visual impact equivalent to suddenly erupting sound. On either side of the bolt Lichtenstein scrupulously orchestrated an interplay of verticals and diagonals, curves and straight edges, and dynamic and static forms and, in sync with Art Deco design principles, arranged his geometric figures in repeating sets of two, three, and four. The result, a vigorous, handsomely

15 Frank Stella (American, born 1936)
Hiraqla III 1968
Polymer and fluorescent polymer on canvas, 10 x 20' (304.8 x 609.6 cm)
Kawamura Memorial Museum of Art, Sakura, Japan

contrived abstraction of evident Art Deco heritage, lends itself to comparisons with the Color Field painting of the same period, Frank Stella's Protractor Series (1967–71) (fig. 15), and—farther removed—Mondrian and other painters of Dutch de Stijl in the 1920s. But the picture offers more entertaining, intrinsic alternatives. If, for instance, we look at *Modern Painting with Bolt* the way we look at Lichtenstein's *Girl with Ball* (p. 4), where a blank canvas ground easily suggests a beach, then the painting takes on implications of figuration. The great streak of lightning might illuminate a synoptic, Cubist-derived view of a storm at sea from one of the great ocean liners of the 1920s and 1930s. The vibrant screen of blue benday dots undulating across the lower part of the picture could be a continuation of the ocean as seen from the three portholes at the bottom and, above, the torqued rectangle of pale-red dots an atmospheric glimpse of sky.

However Lichtenstein may have regarded representational references and this particular painting, he was usually not unhappy with fusions and confusions of abstraction and representation. More significant, what is unquestionably central to the Modern series as a whole is a sense of time at once comic and poignant. Speaking of the Art Deco generation Lichtenstein said, "They believed very much in the rational and logical. To me there is something humorous in being that logical and rational about a work of art." Along these lines he also commented, "They felt they were much more modern than we feel we are now." Thus, as Lawrence Alloway observed, Lichtenstein is "neither nostalgic nor camp, but dealing with human experience in time, as the title of the series, Modern paintings, signals."

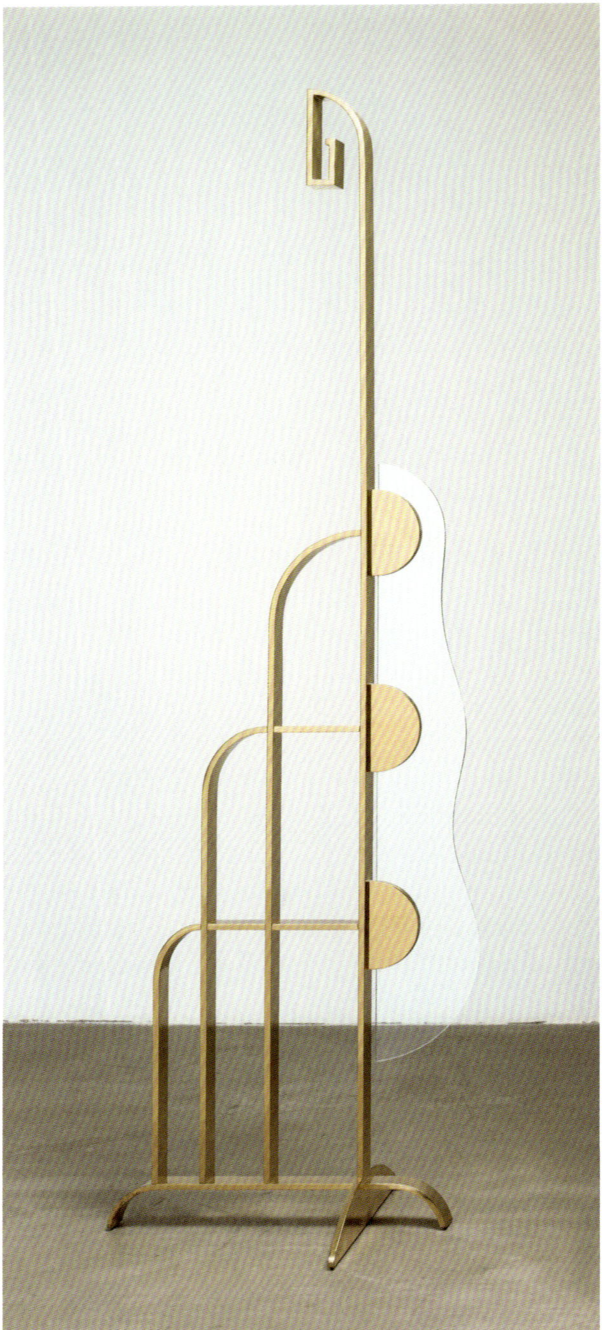

Modern Sculpture with Glass Wave (1967) Like a painting in Lichtenstein's Modern series, *Modern Sculpture with Glass Wave*, from the artist's parallel set of sculptures, is a sampler of the Art Deco style, a single object that sums up a rich tradition. The artist himself compared pieces like this to "swank facades" or, with a casual, still open-ended specificity, to the "portals, and doorways, and banisters" of 1930s design still ubiquitous in New York, Paris, and other Western cities. Given their use of such traditional materials as glass, marble, and brass, there was, he said, nothing unusual about his sculptures; rather, each one looked "like something I found in the lobby of something."

Fair as Lichtenstein's appraisal is, the "finding" was all in his head. His elegantly streamlined pieces that came of certain lobby encounters have no affinities whatsoever with the "found object" school of sculpture being practiced by such contemporaries as Mark di Suvero or Richard Stankiewicz. Rather, Lichtenstein saw a relation between his Art Deco sculpture and Minimalism by way of an operative bond between the artists and designers of the 1930s and his Minimalist peers. The work of both was, he said, "conceptual. . . . The shape that finally evolves is to a great degree understood to begin with." True enough, and true also that Minimalism's rigorously cerebral modes might seem to accommodate the address of a work like *Modern Sculpture with Glass Wave*—linear, open, diagrammatic, and virtually without volume. Yet Minimalism's insistence on absolute abstraction without a hint of external reference bars any meaningful filiation with Lichtenstein's work.

Modern Sculpture with Glass Wave 1967
Brass and glass, 7' 7 1/4" x 29" x 28"
(231.8 x 73.8 x 70.1 cm)
The Museum of Modern Art, New York.
Gift of Mr. and Mrs. Richard L. Selle, 1976

The closest affinity of a piece such as this to another body of work is to the artist's own painting. His objects are, as Lawrence Alloway put it, "anti-sculptural sculpture" inhabited by "a malice towards three dimensionality." In this respect Lichtenstein's temperament was like and unlike that of Alberto Giacometti, a sculptor and painter who made his figures thinner and thinner in order to force the optical effects of illusionist perspective into clay, plaster, and bronze. More straightforwardly, Lichtenstein wanted to drain his sculptures of volume. He wanted them to exist as two-dimensional constructs, frontal with an emphasis on the flat plane. The description he provided of his own experience of his sculpture might be particularly apposite to the gleaming surfaces of *Modern Sculpture with Glass Wave*:

> *Sculpture might have an exterior form and then it has changes within that form which create contrast. . . . Contrast may be in a cast shadow or in the illusion of a cast shadow, or . . . created in any conceivable way. Now, as you turn the sculpture, or move your position, you continually perceive it differently. It's the relationship of contrast to contrast, rather than volume to volume, which makes it work. So, even though I realize it is three-dimensional, it is always a two-dimensional relationship to me—or as two-dimensional as a drawing is.*

Indeed, apart from their very different presentations and the social uses of their subjects, *Modern Sculpture with Glass Wave* shares with such earlier painting/drawings as *Tire* (p. 8) a lean Precisionist articulation that makes the mute object an eloquent means of viewing people through their artifacts.

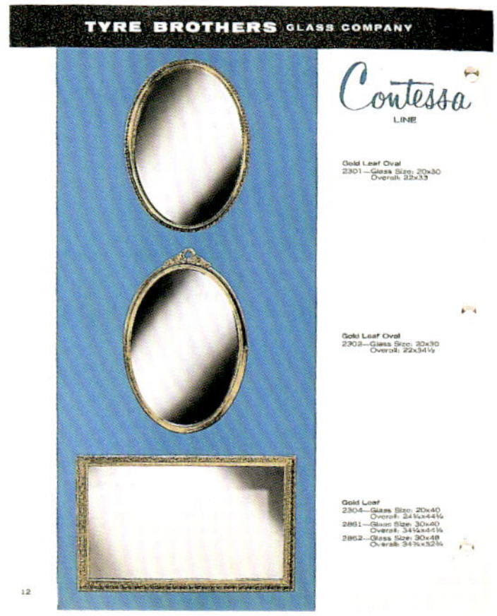

Mirror #10 **(1970)** "With his genius for steering the history of high art into the lowest depths of popular art and then triumphing over the collision," Lichtenstein was, in Robert Rosenblum's view, "destined to take on one of the loftiest motifs of Western painting, the mirror." The artist's rendezvous with destiny took place outside the windows of glass stores in the Bowery on New York's Lower East Side. He was, he recalled, so attracted by the way the brochures on display in their windows (fig. 16) rendered mirrors "with air-brushed mirror symbols, reflecting nothing" that he began making some of his own. Thoroughly conversant with art history, Lichtenstein was probably as much amused as challenged by the contrast between the crass origins of his newly chosen theme and its exalted pedigree in the painted mirrors of Jan Van Eyck, Diego Velázquez, Jean-Auguste-Dominique Ingres, and Édouard Manet, not to mention its celebrated permutations in the work of such twentieth-century masters as Pablo Picasso and Juan Gris.

Mirror #10 is one of a series of fifty or so mirror paintings Lichtenstein produced between late 1969 and 1972. They come

16 Page from an undated Tyre Brothers Glass Company brochure, Los Angeles

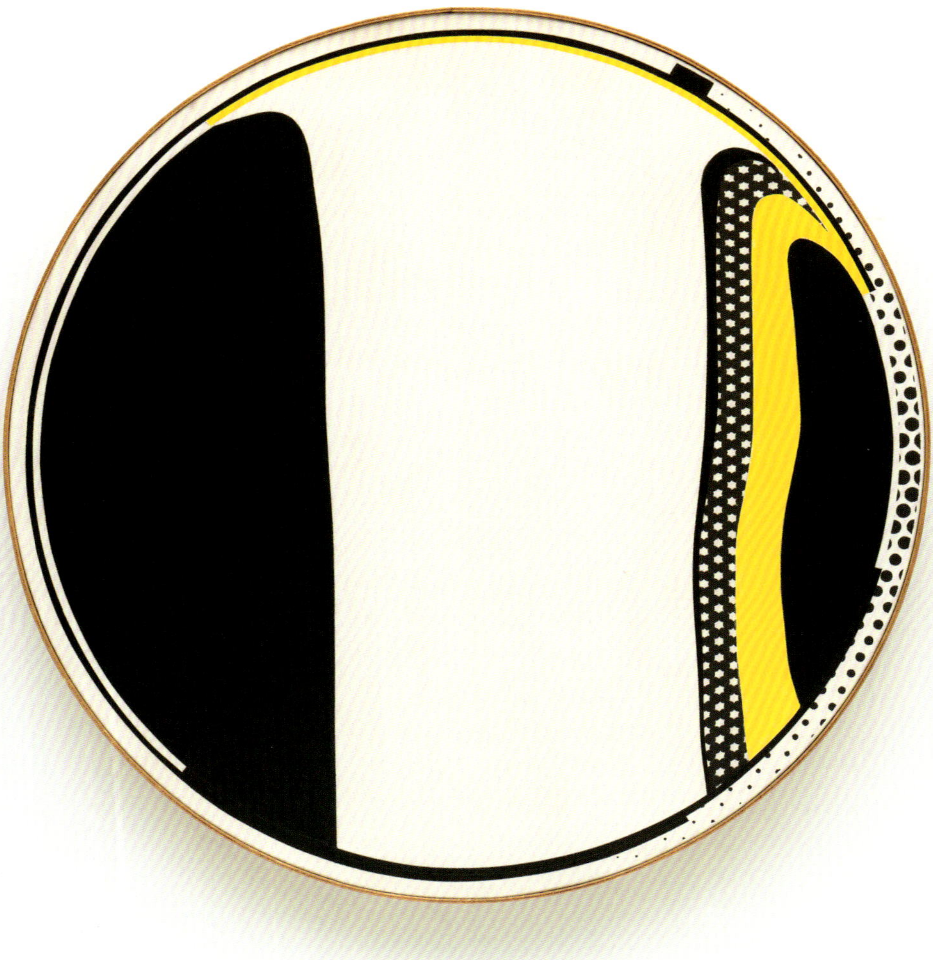

Mirror #10 1970
Oil and synthetic polymer paint on canvas,
24" (61 cm) diam.
The Museum of Modern Art, New York.
Partial and promised gift of UBS, 2002

in varying sizes—from quite small, such as *#10*, to nearly room-size paneled screens—in three invariant formats: circle, oval, and rectangle. Their common denominator, the mirror's face, provoked Lichtenstein to experiment with the abstract potentials of his own style and with abstraction as subject and, along the way, by sly, welcome coincidence, to allude to the art of his contemporaries. A Lichtenstein mirror, with its entire surface identified as subject, operates somewhat like a Jasper Johns map as well as a semifigurative version of the shaped canvases then favored by abstract artists. In their own terms the paintings are, as Elizabeth Baker has put it, "elaborately composed pictures of reflections of air." Their creator, in less than concealed self-reference, claimed, "They really only look like mirrors if someone tells you they do. Only once you know that, they can be moved as far as possible from realism, but you want it to be taken for realism. It becomes as stylized as you can get it." Hardly naive, Lichtenstein knew quite well that titular direction alone would not bring anyone's eye/mind apparatus around to a perception of dull canvas as light-receptive surface. Accordingly, without deviating from the restrictions of his established vocabulary of flat primary colors, white ground, and mechanical, stenciled benday dots, he readjusted its syntax to create abstract imagery of simulated glass and refracted light.

The strategies deployed in *Mirror #10* are typical of Lichtenstein's simple but precisely calculated maneuvering. Here, the graphic conventions by which light reflection is indicated in the brochures establish the painting's structure. A wide, uninterrupted zone of light is defined between the unusually soft-edged mass of planar blackness to the left and its complementary, more lively shadow to the right. Sensations of flickering light and the visual feel of dazzling yellow shimmer are mostly generated by Lichtenstein's new willingness to adjust his screens of dots. In *Mirror #10* their nearly uniform size and irregular contours in the outside band of black to the right contrasts with their symmetrically repeated movement from small to large on the painting's perimeter, creating an immediately recognizable optical code for mirrored glimpses of patterned light in dark shadow and the tilting plane of a beveled edge. Like this one, Lichtenstein's paintings in tondo form tend to be compositionally spare and coloristically assertive—often favoring dramatic juxtapositions of black, white, and yellow. Slick, classy, and oddly period specific, *Mirror #10* is both abstract painting and surrogate object. Arrested on its surface is a blank, ephemeral moment that never was—late afternoon, late 1930, Malibu? The other coast? It's viewer's choice.

Artist's Studio "The Dance" (1974)

Lichtenstein described this painting as the most lyrical of the five large paintings in the Artist's Studio series he made in 1973 and 1974. Loaded with historical mystique, the theme of the artist's workplace was the perfect choice at a moment when Lichtenstein wanted to reverse his methods—to exchange his customary conversion of low art to high style for a process of taking on high

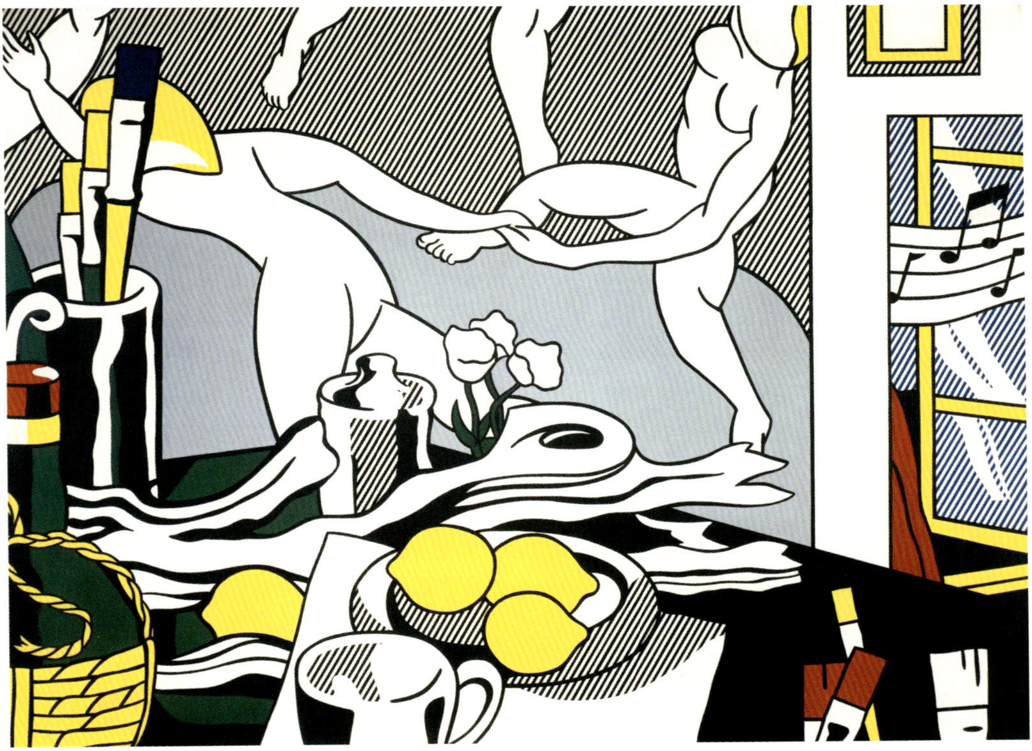

Artist's Studio "The Dance" 1974
Oil and synthetic polymer paint on canvas,
8' 1/8" x 10' 8 1/8" (244.3 x 325.5 cm)
The Museum of Modern Art, New York.
Gift of Mr. and Mrs. S. I. Newhouse, Jr., 1990

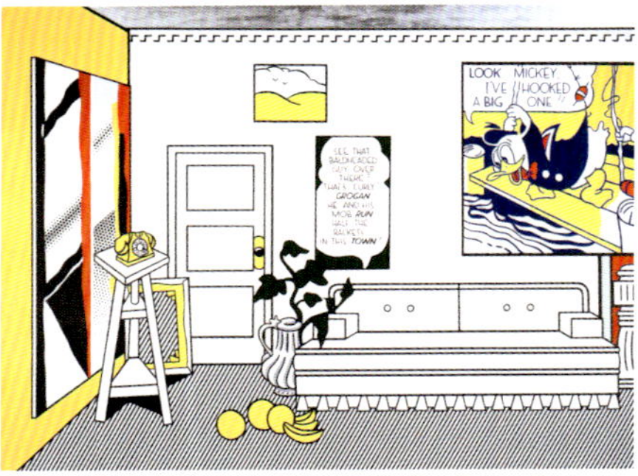

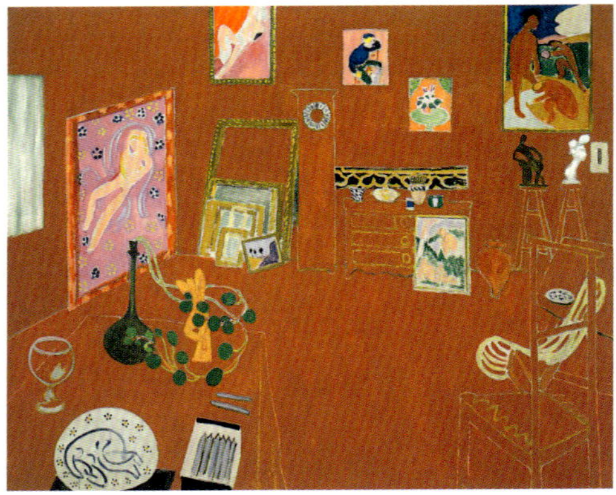

style to get to high-style-as-subject. Coming upon reproductions of several paintings by Henri Matisse, he found an ideal, if posthumously enlisted, collaborator. In all five paintings of the new series the artist's studio is an interior where Lichtenstein and the French master keep company. It was an "audacity," Lawrence Alloway observed, "condoned by the market," and by "Lichtenstein's view of art as an array of provisional and deceptive signs in a continually unsettled state."

Consonant with this understanding of art as an open resource, Lichtenstein variously borrowed from Matisse. In *Artist's Studio No. 1 (Look Mickey)* (fig. 17) he devised a studio of distinctly peculiar allure on the structural principles of Matisse's magisterial *Red Studio* of 1911 (fig. 18). The model was astutely selected. By the time Lichtenstein began skirmishing with it, the painting's fame and status were legendary. No other twentieth-century painter had so memorably presented the studio space as a gallery to exhibit the works produced within it. It was also without peer in a domain that would have particularly interested Lichtenstein, being, as pronounced by Clement Greenberg, "the flattest painting done anywhere up to that time." Time,

17 *Artist's Studio No. 1 (Look Mickey)* 1973
Oil, Magna, and sand on canvas,
8' 1/8" x 10' 6 1/8" (244.2 x 325.4 cm)
Collection Walker Art Center, Minneapolis.
Gift of Judy and Kenneth Dayton and the
T. B. Walker Foundation, 1981

18 Henri Matisse (French, 1869–1954)
The Red Studio 1911
Oil on canvas, 71 1/4" x 7' 2 1/4"
(181 x 219.1 cm)
The Museum of Modern Art, New York.
Mrs. Simon Guggenheim Fund, 1949

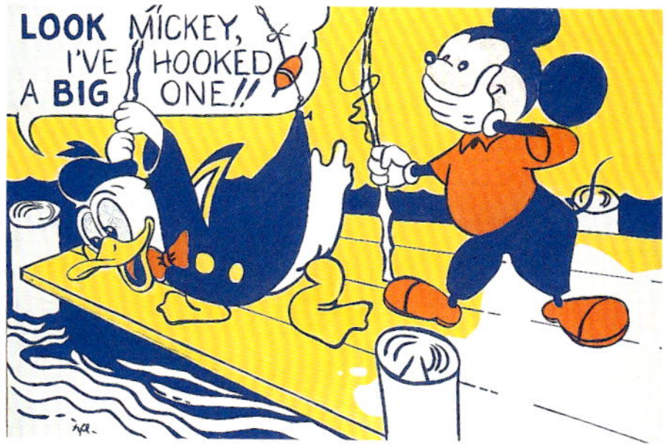

of course, had gone by, and the issue of pictorial flatness had become highly fraught, to say the least. More than likely, Lichtenstein enjoyed a bit of affectionate, naughty-boy delight in revamping Matisse's studio into a suitable showcase for the display of *Look Mickey*, his "first" (he said) Pop painting (fig. 19). In the original, Matisse had allowed some ghost-thin lines to hint at recessive space but otherwise had abolished almost all traces of three-dimensional illusionism. Nonetheless, the tilt of stacked canvases leaning obliquely against the studio walls together with the all-enveloping, Rothko-like film of sensate color establishes an overall feeling of penetrable space. In Lichtenstein's unnaturally white, diagrammatic version, perspectival coordinates are forthrightly indicated, but the resulting rectilinear architecture only reinforces the room's flatness, made still more apparent by the regimented diagonals tipping the floor toward the picture plane. Although Lichtenstein ruthlessly redefined the comparatively capacious space of his source, he was appropriately respectful in decorating the denatured product. Only the picture's emblematic philodendron and telephone stand refer to Matisse. With the exception of a detail from a painting by

19 *Look Mickey* 1961
Oil on canvas, 48 x 69" (121.9 x 175.3 cm)
National Gallery of Art, Washington, D.C.
Dorothy and Roy Lichtenstein. Gift of the Artist, in Honor of the 50th Anniversary of the National Gallery of Art

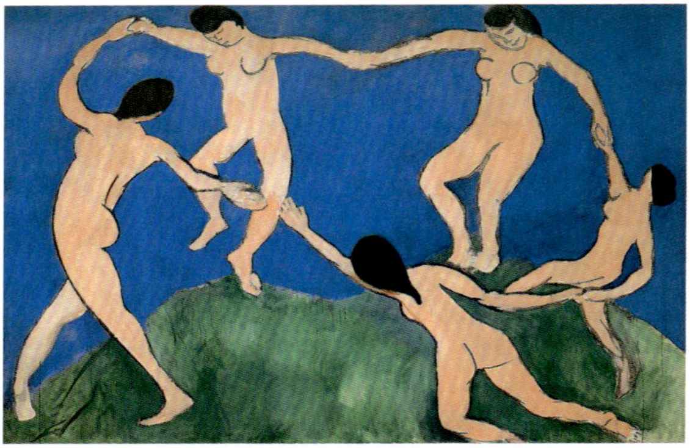

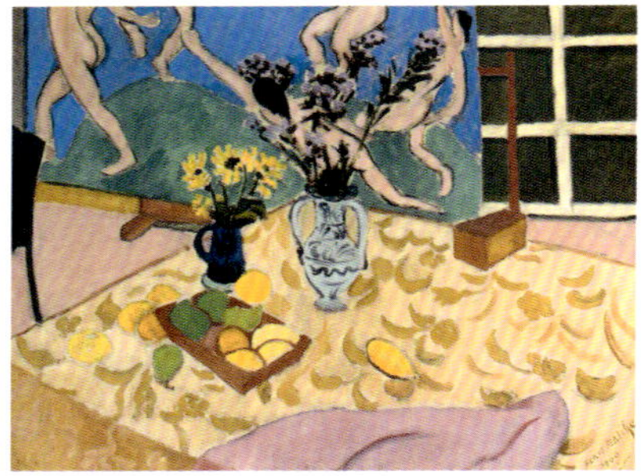

Fernand Léger beneath the truncated right side of *Look Mickey*, all the other objects in the room, including the phone and door, are from his own art.

If Matisse's contribution to *Artist's Studio No. 1 (Look Mickey)* largely consists of historical aura and an enabling pictorial architecture, his presence is the immediate animating force, structurally and figuratively, in *Artist's Studio "The Dance."* The centrality and prominence given to Matisse's famous dancers—of *Dance (I)* and *(II)*, from 1909 and 1910 (figs. 20 and 23)—will likely cause most viewers of Lichtenstein's painting to see his revelers as their direct descendents. In fact they are collateral, and the whole painting is based on a related Matisse of 1909, *Still Life with "Dance"* (fig. 21). Although Lichtenstein remained his own man in terms of color, deploying the same palette of primaries plus green, white, and black he had in *Artist's Studio No. 1 (Look Mickey)*, this time his picture is a close variant of its model. Aside from his signature stylization, a proportional compressing of canvas size, and the addition of a considerable number of props, he retained the laterally spreading advance of tilted triangular tabletop into the field of the dancers—while avoiding, as did Matisse, any visual indication of discontinuous planarity.

20 Henri Matisse (French, 1869–1954)
Dance (I) 1909
Oil on canvas, 8' 6 1/2" x 12' 9 1/2" (259.7 x 390.1 cm)
The Museum of Modern Art, New York. Gift of Nelson A. Rockefeller in honor of Alfred H. Barr, Jr., 1963

21 Henri Matisse (French, 1869–1954)
Still Life with "Dance" 1909
Oil on canvas, 35 x 45 5/8" (89 x 116 cm)
The State Hermitage Museum, St. Petersburg

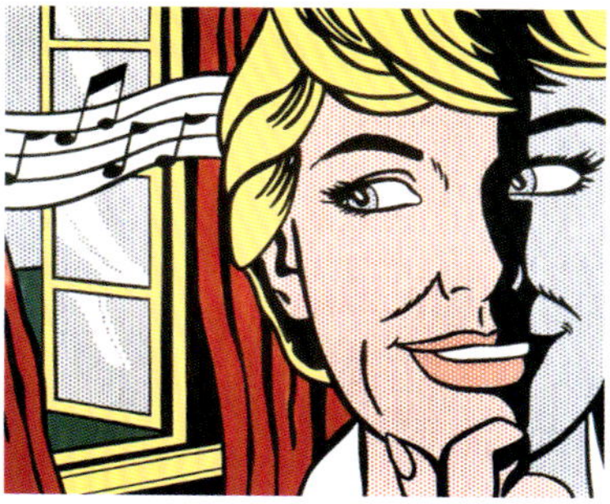

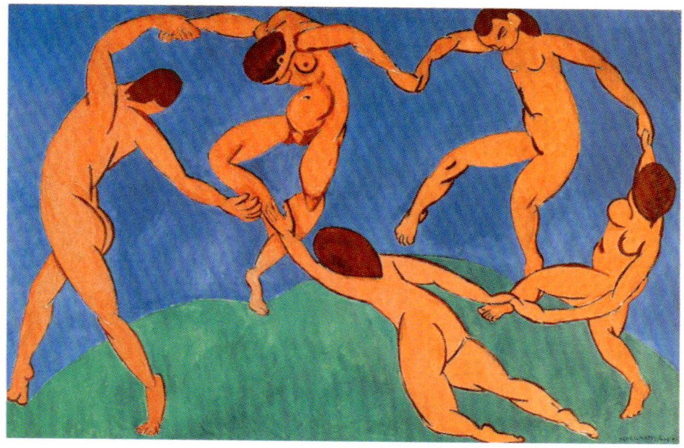

Giving relatively short shrift to his own art, he replaced Matisse's mullioned window on the right with a window and musical notes borrowed from his own *Sound of Music* of 1964 (fig. 22)—thus these once arcadian ladies dance to a tune out of a popular movie. It could be that the driftwood on the table is an albino echo of Lichtenstein's brushstroke sculptures; however intended, its white, elastically undulant forms stretching into the limbs of the dancers enhance a sense of their exuberant movement. Their figures offer creditable evidence that Lichtenstein was interested in the *how* of their dancing: of the two versions of *Dance* Matisse made in 1909 and 1910 the first is far more like the dancers in *Still Life with "Dance,"* the painting Lichtenstein used as his model, yet the sinewy, tightly energetic dancers in his *Artist's Studio "The Dance"* derive unequivocally from the second; given their starring role in his painting, it is reasonable to assume that Lichtenstein chose the second group for their superior dancing. The curious contrast between such close attention to the details of Matisse's styling in *Artist's Studio "The Dance"* and their virtual obliteration in *Artist's Studio No. 1 (Look Mickey)* may have to do with Lichtenstein's will to negotiate a balance with his models. Perhaps the ludicrously stripped-down atelier in *Artist's*

22 *Sound of Music* 1964
Oil and Magna on canvas, 48 x 56"
(121.9 x 142.2 cm)
Collection Barbara and Richard S. Lane

23 Henri Matisse (French, 1869–1954)
Dance (II) 1909–10
Oil on canvas, 8' 5 5/8" x 12' 9 1/2"
(260 x 391 cm)
The State Hermitage Museum, St. Petersburg.
Formerly collection Sergei Shchukin

Studio No. 1 (Look Mickey) constitutes a late-twentieth-century cartoonish approximation and appreciation of *The Red Studio*'s outrageous radicality circa 1911; whereas the more comfortable, "lyrical" locale of *Artist's Studio "The Dance"* takes its character from Matisse's earlier traditional still life.

Glass IV (1976)

During the three-plus decades since Lichtenstein made *Glass IV*, sculpture has become so adventuresome that its capacity to surprise has diminished. Nonetheless, despite its age and some extravagant competition, *Glass IV* remains quietly startling. Where Lichtenstein's deadpan treatment of humdrum objects (see *Tire*, p. 8, for example) in his single-image paintings of the early 1960s had invested them with a kind of goofy dignity and monolithic presence, in the late 1970s, when he began using the same sort of things to make sculptures, the resulting effects were, to borrow a kindergarten locution, the same but different. In *Glass IV* goofiness cedes to sophisticated humor and the monolithic yields to the diffuse in a sculpture whose elegant poise raises the kitchen glass to the level of contemplation once accorded a horse and rider but, at the time of its making, more often given to a kind of abstract sculpture referred to as "drawing in air." In fact, that phrase—minus the inferred abstraction—is not an inapt description of this five-feet-tall bronze drinking glass designed to refer not only to its author's black-and-white images of the early 1960s but to a range of other paintings, notably the 1970s Mirror series and some exactly contemporaneous still lifes.

Glass IV 1976
Painted bronze, 49 x 29 3/4 x 14 7/8"
(124.3 x 75.5 x 37.8 cm)
The Museum of Modern Art, New York.
Gift of Ellsworth Kelly, 1999

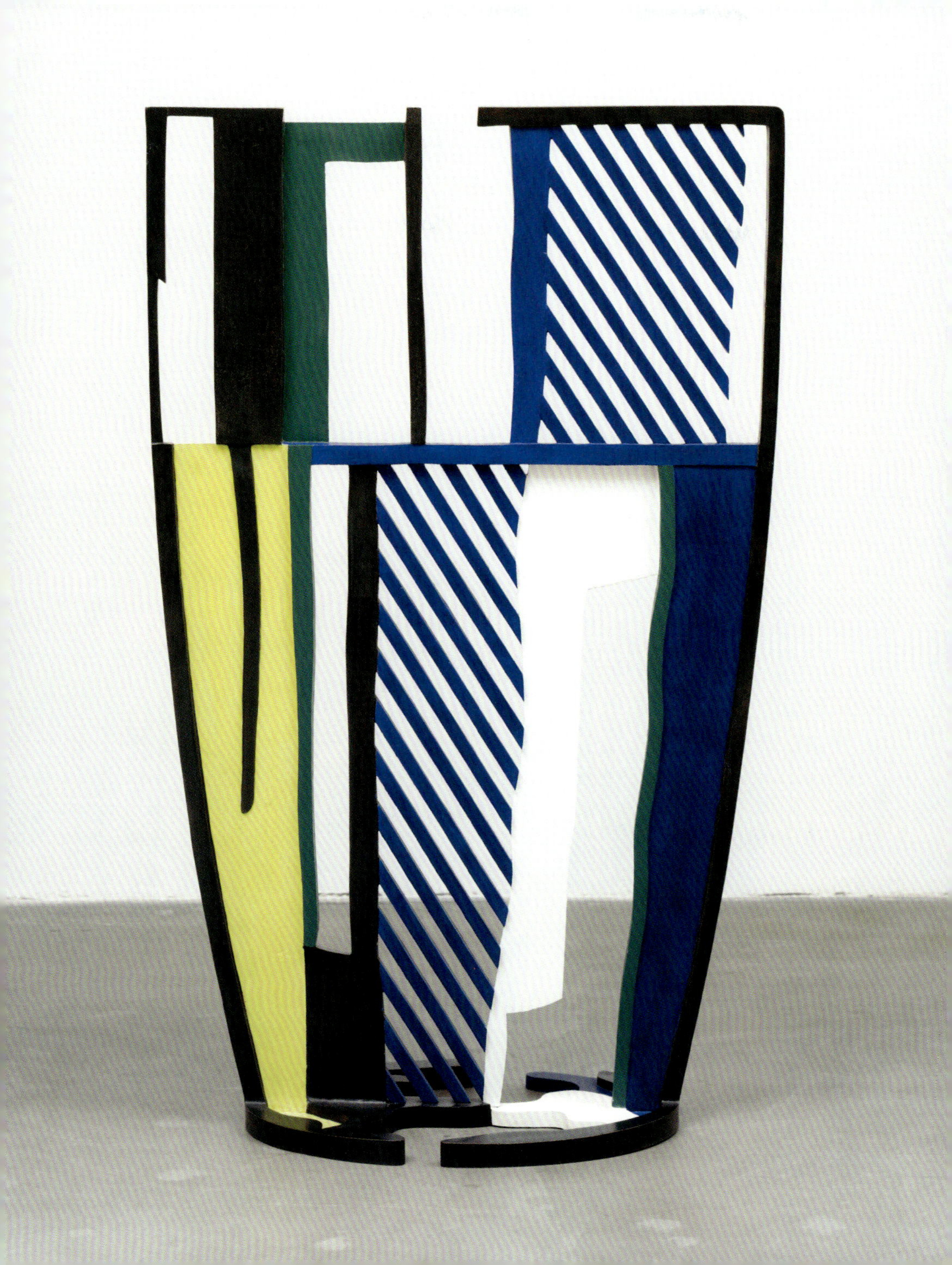

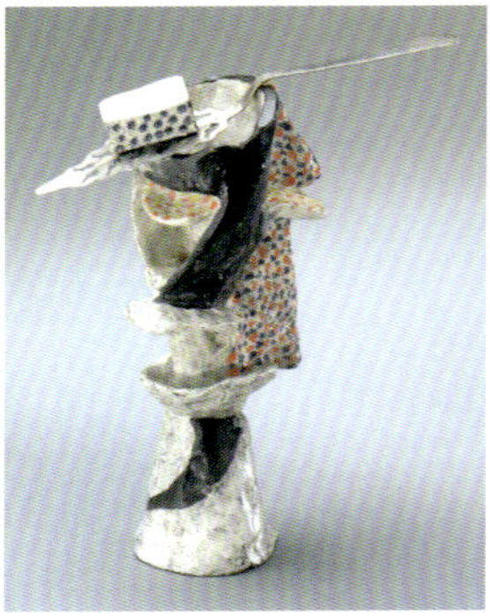

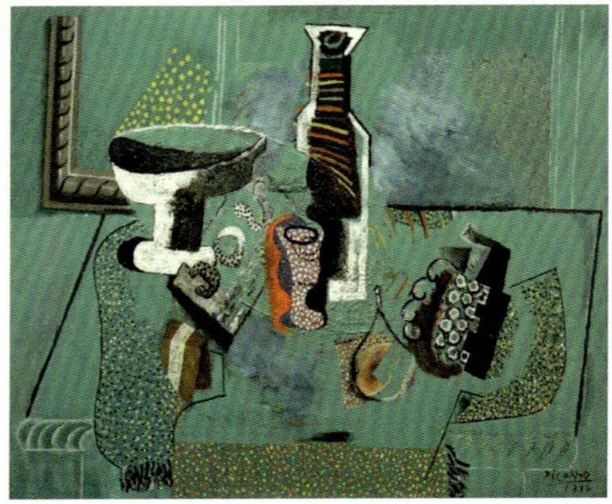

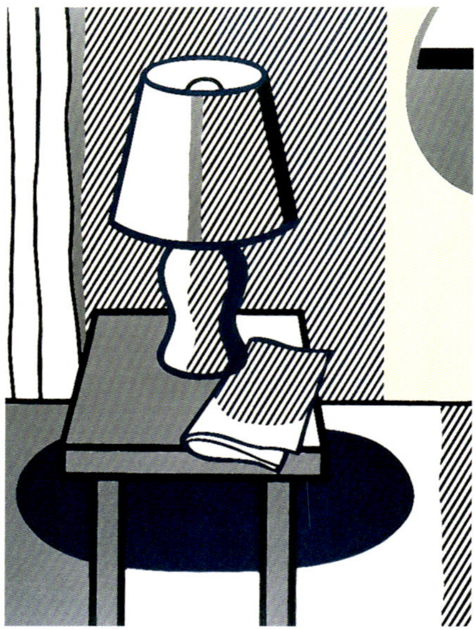

24 Pablo Picasso (Spanish, 1881–1973)
Glass of Absinthe 1914
Painted bronze with absinthe spoon, 8 1/2 x 6 1/2 x 3 3/8" (21.6 x 16.4 x 8.5 cm), diam. at base 2 1/2" (6.4 cm)
The Museum of Modern Art, New York. Gift of Louise Reinhardt Smith, 1956

25 Pablo Picasso (Spanish, 1881–1973)
Green Still Life 1914
Oil on canvas, 23 1/2 x 31 1/4" (59.7 x 79.4 cm)
The Museum of Modern Art, New York. Lillie P. Bliss Collection, 1934

Bottom:
26 *Still Life with Table Lamp* 1976
Oil and Magna on canvas, 6' 2" x 54" (187.9 x 137.2 cm)
Private collection

Assigning *Glass IV* and other such sculptures functions associated with paintings, Lichtenstein paid no heed to the doctrine preached to his generation that each medium should remain within its "legitimate boundaries." Contemporary canon notwithstanding, Lichtenstein's happy disregard for its dictates had long since been sanctioned by Pablo Picasso's *Glass of Absinthe* of 1914 (fig. 24), which demonstrates that a certain kind of stippled brushwork emphasizes the surface of an object in a painting (fig. 25) and tends to dissolve it in a sculpture. A very similar set of crossover tactics is at play between *Glass IV* and *Still Life with Table Lamp*, also of 1976 (fig. 26). In the latter, using one of his favorite signs for impressions of light and shadow—widely spaced diagonals mostly in black or dark blue—Lichtenstein selectively articulates the surfaces of wall and objects in the still life through his chosen decorative code. Transcribing it in *Glass IV*, he opted for actual transparency. The diagonals of the long central "plane" and the shorter one above, to the left, are alternately bronze and air, a real-world translation of figure and ground. That interaction plays to each side of the striped panels in sudden jumps between positive form and negative space, in flexible exchanges between the two- and three-dimensional, and in arch confusions between the real and the fictive. *Glass IV*, an immensely savvy, amusing theater of pictorial and sculptural dynamics, is a kind of genial *trompe l'oeil* not so much interested in deceiving the eye as entertaining it.

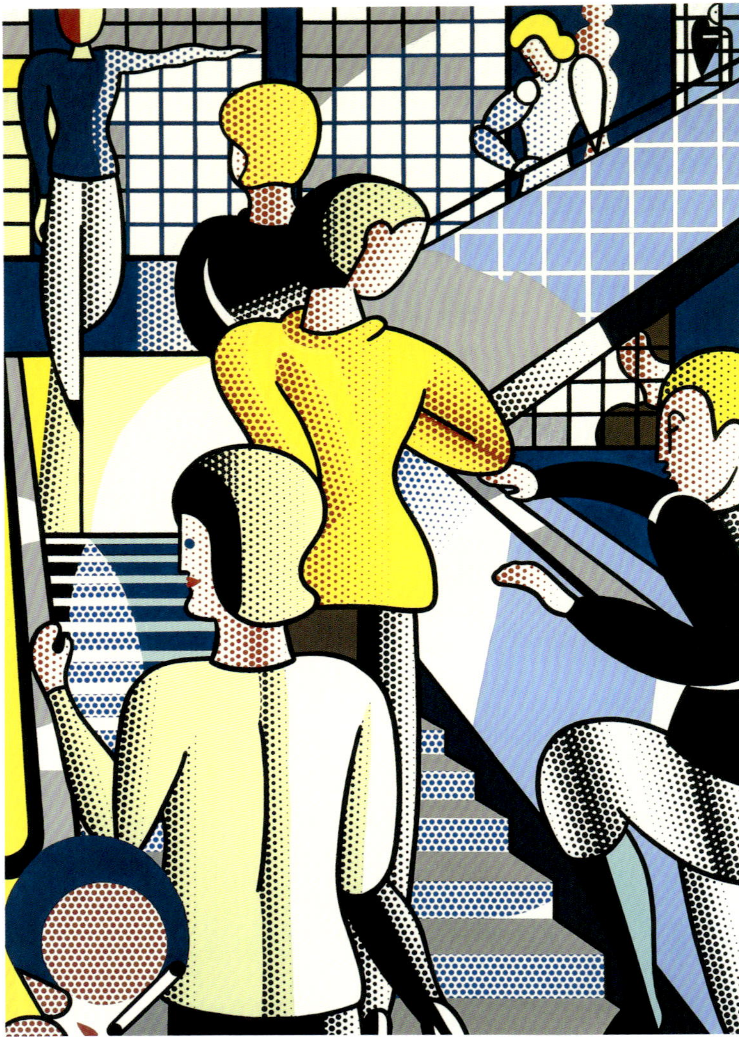

Bauhaus Stairway 1988
Oil and synthetic polymer paint on canvas,
7' 10" x 66" (238.8 x 167.7 cm)
The Museum of Modern Art, New York.
Gift of Dorothy and Roy Lichtenstein, 1990

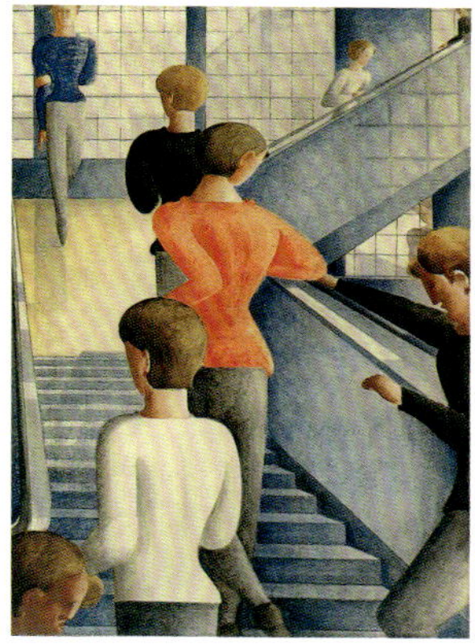

Bauhaus Stairway (1988)

By the time Lichtenstein made *Bauhaus Stairway*—after Oskar Schlemmer's 1932 painting of the same title (fig. 27)—he was a practiced hand at the quotation and paraphrase of older, mostly twentieth-century European artists. For the most part, his chosen models were such renowned masters as Matisse, Picasso, and Mondrian, but less prominent Futurists, Surrealists, and German Expressionists also served. While Schlemmer was influential in Germany and one of the more important masters teaching at the Bauhaus school during the 1920s, his work in general was not widely known. That being said, Lichtenstein, whose knowledge of art history has been called encyclopedic, was almost undoubtedly aware of Schlemmer and likely felt some kinship with the German artist's emotional cool and the rigorous balance he maintained between formal purity and representational imagery. The most significant impetus to Lichtenstein's manufacture of his own Schlemmer was, however, not distant knowledge but the hometown iconic status of the original, which had been hanging in a replica of the real Bauhaus stairwell at The Museum of Modern Art in New York for years.

27 Oskar Schlemmer (German, 1888–1943)
Bauhaus Stairway 1932
Oil on canvas, 63 7/8 x 45" (162.3 x 114.3 cm)
The Museum of Modern Art, New York. Gift of Philip Johnson, 1942

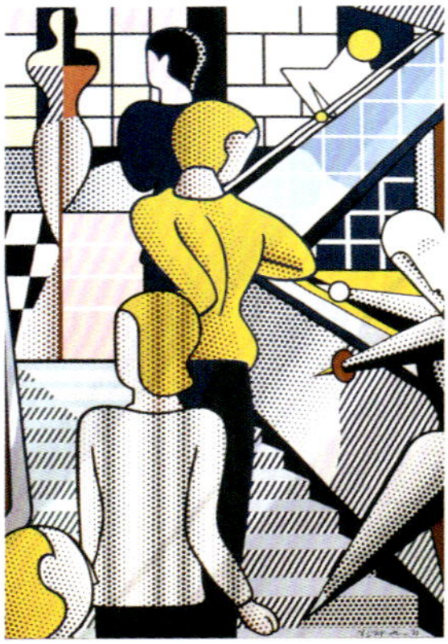

When Lichtenstein painted his version of *Bauhaus Stairway*, his usual inclination to bend the model to his own critical ends seems to have been in partial abeyance. Disparities between his canvas and Schlemmer's are minimal. The Lichtenstein is significantly bigger, but its proportions nearly match those of the Schlemmer. With the exception of the man entering at the lower right, the woman directly above him, and the androgynous figure at the upper left, the attitudes of the stair climbers are virtually identical and the staircase itself largely unrevised. Schlemmer's palette was uncommonly hospitable—all Lichtenstein had to do to make it his own was clean up its smudgy variants of the primaries and add, in relatively large doses, his signature saturated yellow. It may be that he provided the woman at the lower left with a face to get a little extra compositional zip from the unadulterated red of her lips. Just as he keyed up Schlemmer's colors, he smartened up the architecture, intensifying its geometric angles with black outlines like those emphasizing the curvilinear forms of the stair climbers' bodies. The most striking deviation from the original is Lichtenstein's deployment of benday dots in graduated sizes to articulate the forms in frozen progression through fixed zones of light and shadow.

28 *Bauhaus Stairway: The Large Version* 1989
Oil and Magna on canvas, 27 x 18' (8.2 x 5.5 cm)
Creative Artists Agency, Beverly Hills, California.
Collection Michael Ovitz

The Schlemmer, too, provides a sense of stasis, of mannequinlike figures arrested in the atmosphere of a long-ago moment. Much of that bittersweet nostalgia arises from its historical baggage, but not all. It is a highly stylized picture made by a Master of Form of the Bauhaus theater who favored turning performers into living sculptures integrated with their surroundings. As for Lichtenstein, his *Bauhaus Stairway* is an intensely dynamic tribute to Schlemmer and his ambitions. A year after its completion he picked up the theme again—this time for a mural whose further revisions of the original incorporate figures who share space with a helmeted dancer from the German master's *Triadic Ballet* (fig. 28).

Interior with Mobile (1992)

Contrived with consummate cunning, this room-size, relentlessly flat bedroom delivers a stunning visual impact. Neither description nor photography can adequately approximate its sheer optical voltage. Tame enough as a theme, the domestic interior had interested Lichtenstein since such paintings as *Bathroom* of 1961 (fig. 29). Here, thirty years and many interiors later, he is not done with the subject and is still imposing high style on images found in low-end commercial advertising (fig. 30). Now, however, the synthesis of these opposed worlds of visual experience is effected with dazzling panache.

There is about the picture a kind of deranged rationality, both formal and iconographic. Hugging every depicted object—the sole exception the blatantly artificial greenery on the dresser—

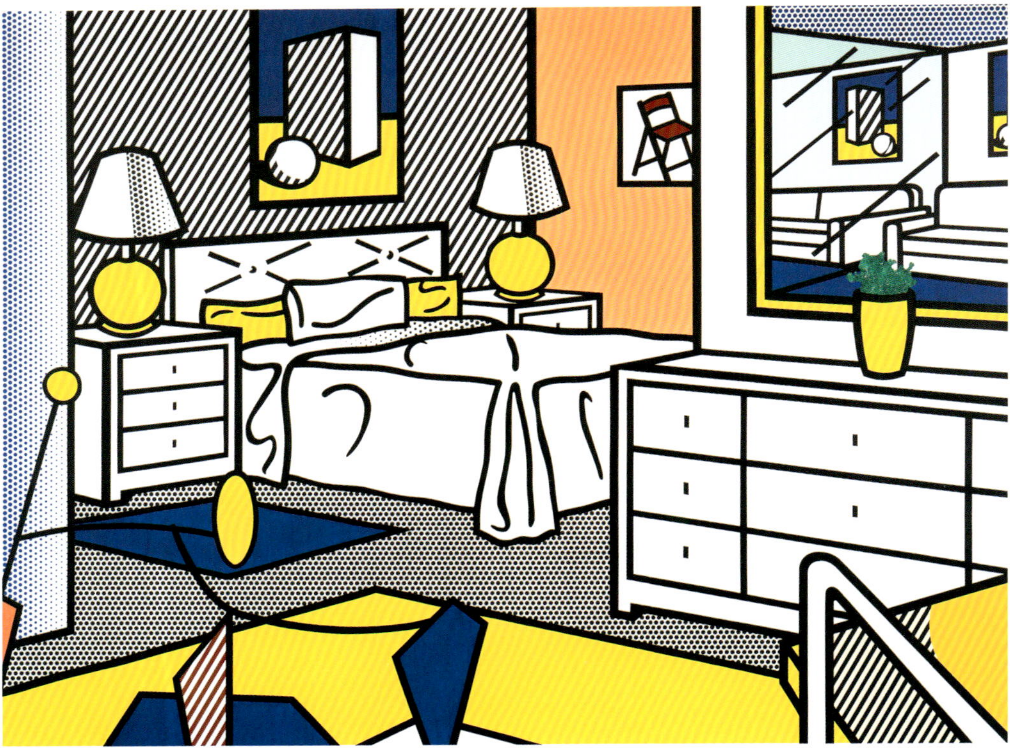

Interior with Mobile 1992
Oil and synthetic polymer paint on canvas,
10' 10" x 14' 3" (330.2 x 434.4 cm)
The Museum of Modern Art, New York. Enid A. Haupt Fund; gift of Agnes Gund, Jo Carole and Ronald S. Lauder, Michael and Judy Ovitz in honor of Roy and Dorothy Lichtenstein, and Anna Marie and Robert F. Shapiro, 1992

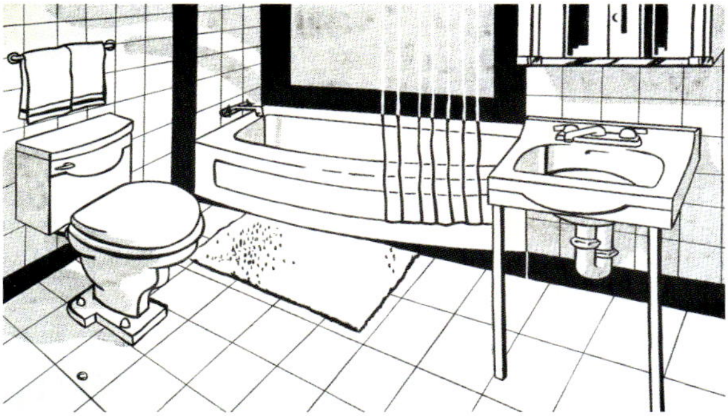

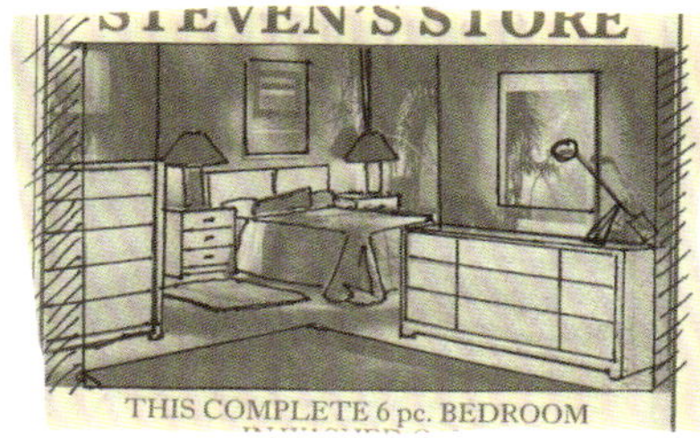

Lichtenstein's signature black outline literally locks together everything but the paintings on the walls and defines their spatial positions in the room. But that same denominator of front, back, and in-between acts in concert with color and shape to keep depth and surface in constant play. In conventional perspective the high-keyed triangle of yellow rug at the bottom should lead into the picture, which to some degree it does, but in interaction with the bedroom's other objects of exactly the same color it loses, if not reverses, momentum. In leftward staccato rhythm from the yellow round of the lamp base at center, through the oddly louche pillows at each end of the headboard, to the second lamp base, to the rhyming circle and oval elements sticking up like Peeping Toms from the partially displayed Alexander Calder mobile at the bottom, a visual pressure builds to tip the rug up, to make its chevron shape level with the complementary blunt geometry of the yellow area in the picture hanging over the bed.

Interior with Mobile does not want the eye to settle down. Rather it encourages jumps from the mock shadows of graduated benday dots on the lamps and left wall to their even distribution on the floor, from the regimented diagonals surrounding

29 *Bathroom* 1961
Oil on canvas, 45 3/4 x 69 1/4" (116.2 x 175.9 cm)
Whitney Museum of American Art, New York. Gift of the American Contemporary Art Foundation, Inc., Leonard A. Lauder, President

30 *Study for Interior with Mobile* 1991
Cut-and-pasted newspaper on notebook paper with felt-tip pen, 4 x 6 1/2" (10.2 x 16.5 cm)
The Museum of Modern Art, New York. Gift of the artist, 1992

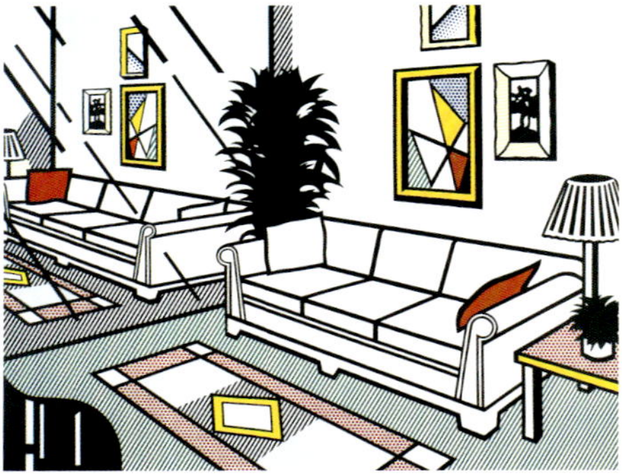

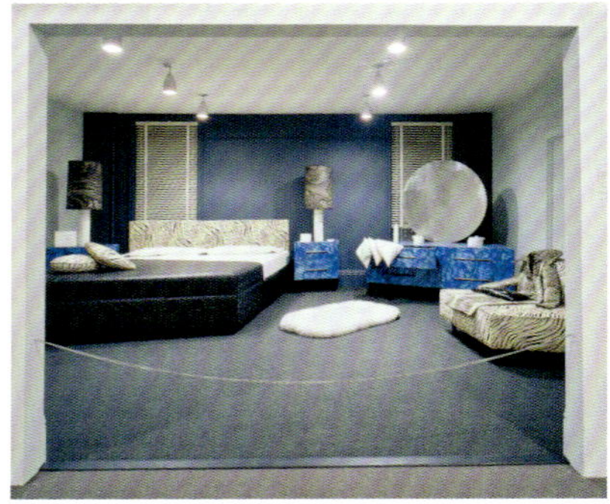

the bed to their repetition in solemn spoofs of high geometric abstraction—once in the picture hanging over the bed and twice again in another over the dresser. This last, a picture-within-a-picture, throws in another visual curve, semi-masquerading as a mirror reflecting a painting while it is, in pictorial fact, a painting incorporating a mirror on the order of *Interior with Mirrored Wall* of the previous year (fig. 31). To ward off the monotony an unrelieved angularity might impose, the double bed, whose edge is equally the rigid left corner of the dresser, is described in free-form squiggles that reach back to Surrealism among many other forms of high twentieth-century art. Above, in the bed's headboard, its one rigidly described appurtenance, two upholstery dimples glare like furious eyes out at the room. Perhaps they are furiously trying to decipher the visual high jinx surrounding them.

An obvious if distanced precedent for *Interior with Mobile* is Claes Oldenburg's *Bedroom Ensemble* of about thirty years earlier (fig. 32). In very different ways, both are stage sets for critical mix-ups of the rational and the irrational, the hard and the soft, the common and the refined. Among the intersecting strategies of the two bedrooms is decoration. In Oldenburg's, fake

31 *Interior with Mirrored Wall* 1991
Oil and Magna on canvas, 10' 4 1/8" x 13' 4"
(320.4 x 406.4 cm)
Solomon R. Guggenheim Museum, New York

32 Claes Oldenburg
(American, born Sweden 1929)
Bedroom Ensemble 1963
Wood, vinyl, metal, artificial fur, cloth, and paper, 9' 11 1/4" x 17' x 21'
(302.9 x 518.2 x 640.1 cm)
National Gallery of Canada, Ottawa

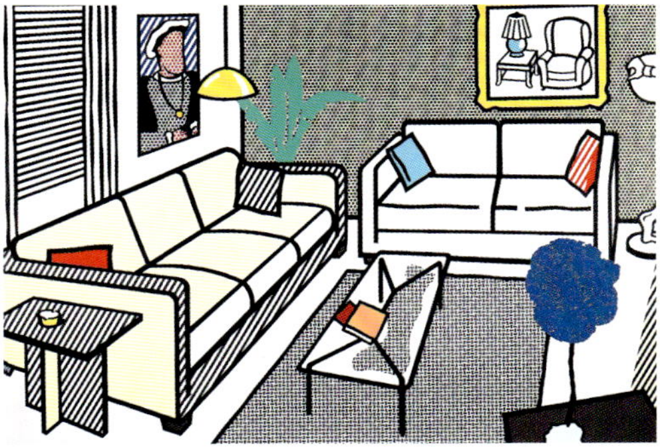

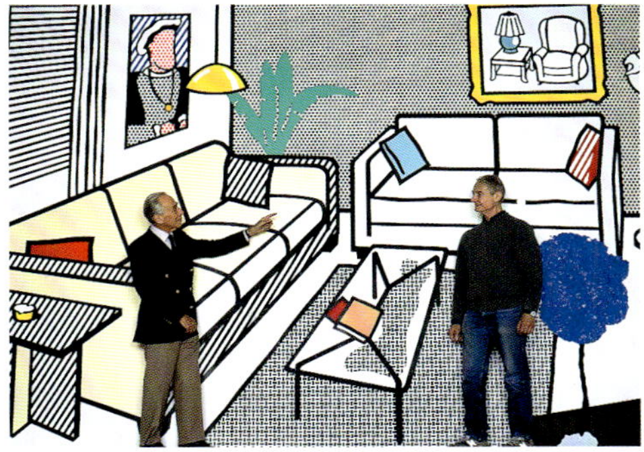

Jackson Pollock paintings ornament the room; in Lichtenstein's a Calder mobile keeps company with his own wacky version of decorator decor and a portrait of a folding chair. In another painting of the same series, *Interior with Yves Klein Sculpture* (fig. 33), a Klein-blue sponge sculpture, a portrait of Henry VIII, another of a dumpy chair and side table, and a life-size reproduction of a Greek discus thrower disappearing off the right edge are all tastefully brought together.

Stylistic discord is present in every painting in Lichtenstein's Interior series, whether as good-humored if highly barbed commentary on postmodern gullibility or as structurally posed puzzles about reflection and illusion, fiction and reality. Diane Waldman has compared them to "the Looking-Glass room" Lewis Carroll provided for Alice. Roberta Smith has said that these works are so inviting one wants to walk right in, like "actors entering Toontown in [the film] 'Who Framed Roger Rabbit.'" That instrument that doesn't lie, the camera, shows us two people who seem to have done so—Leo Castelli and Roy Lichtenstein (fig. 34).

33 *Interior with Yves Klein Sculpture* 1991
Oil and Magna on canvas, 12' x 14' 2 1/4"
(304.8 x 432.4 cm)
Private collection

34 Leo Castelli and Roy Lichtenstein in front of *Interior with Yves Klein Sculpture*, 1991

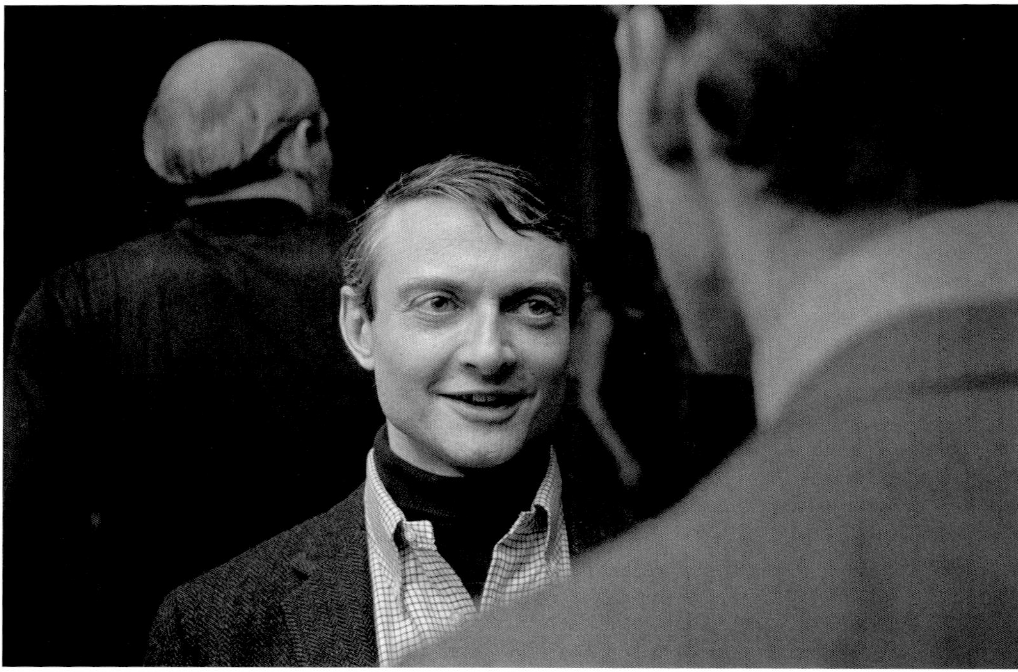

Roy Lichtenstein, New York, 1966

Roy Fox Lichtenstein was born in New York City in 1923. Before and after military service in the 1940s, he studied then taught at the School of Fine Arts at Ohio State University. In 1960, while teaching at Rutgers University, he met Allan Kaprow, whose use of the familiar objects of mass culture in his performance-based art was a decisive influence. By then Lichtenstein had been exhibiting his paintings for ten years and was well versed in Abstract Expressionism. Moving away from the highly personal, emotive abstraction of that dominant mode, he began using imagery from comic strips and advertising in large-scale paintings. Emulating the bold black outlines and bright primary colors of these sources along with print's halftone dots, he created a visual syntax new to American art, one that employed cultural clichés to challenge the aesthetic clichés of high art. His 1962 solo show at the Leo Castelli Gallery is a landmark event in the history of Pop art.

As Lichtenstein's career expanded, so did the scale and mode of his work. Over the next three decades he made public murals, outdoor sculptures, and films, while continuing to draw and paint. He was a classicist at heart, and he went on to treat the full range of twentieth-century modern styles, including Art Deco, Cubism, Futurism, Surrealism, and Expressionism—always with an exquisite precision of optical effect and his trademark sense of humor and the absurd. Lichtenstein's early merging of popular imagery and high art together with his later transgressions of traditional aesthetics makes him one of contemporary art's most challenging and enduring figures. He died in New York in 1997.

Produced by
The Department of Publications,
The Museum of Modern Art, New York

Edited by Rebecca Roberts
Designed by Amanda Washburn
Production by Elisa Frohlich

Printed and bound by Oceanic
Graphic Printing, Inc., China
Typeset in Avenir
Printed on 140 gsm Gold East Matte
Artpaper

Library of Congress Catalogue Card
Number: 2009927224
ISBN: 978-0-87070-770-4

Published by
The Museum of Modern Art
11 West 53 Street
New York NY 10019-5497
www.moma.org

Distributed in the United States and
Canada by D.A.P./Distributed Art
Publishers, Inc.
155 Sixth Avenue, 2nd Floor
New York NY 10013
www.artbook.com

Distributed outside the United States
and Canada by Thames & Hudson, Ltd.
181 High Holborn
London WC1V 7QX
www.thamesandhudson.com

Printed in China

Photograph Credits

All works of art by Roy Lichtenstein © 2009 Estate of Roy Lichtenstein

© 2009 Bob Adelman: 2, 44; © 2009 Artists Rights Society (ARS), New York/ADAGP, Paris: 10 (right); © 2009 DC Comics: 13 (right); © 2009 Succession H. Matisse, Paris/Artists Rights Society (ARS), New York: 28 (right), 30 (left and right), 31 (right); © 2009 Claes Oldenburg: 9 (right), 42 (right); © 2009 Estate of Pablo Picasso/Artists Rights Society (ARS), New York: 7, 34 (top left and right); © 2009 Frank Stella/Artists Rights Society (ARS), New York: 18; © 2009 Andy Warhol Foundation for the Visual Arts/Artists Rights Society (ARS), New York: 9 (left)

Bob Adelman: 2, 38, 44; courtesy The Butler Institute of American Art: 6 (right); Department of Imaging Services, The Museum of Modern Art: 33, 34 (top left), Thomas Griesel: 20, 28 (right), 30 (left), 40, Kate Keller: 4, 9 (right), 12, 27, 34 (top right), 36, 37, Kate Keller/Mali Olatunji: 7, Paige Knight: 16, 24, 41 (right); courtesy Solomon R. Guggenheim Museum, New York: 42 (left); courtesy Kawamura Memorial Museum of Art, Sakura, Japan: 18; courtesy The Collection Kröller-Müller Museum, Otter, the Netherlands: 10 (bottom left); courtesy Estate of Roy Lichtenstein: 5, 10 (top left), 13 (left), 17 (left and right), 23, 31 (left), 34 (bottom), 43 (both); Robert McKeever: 43 (right); courtesy The Metropolitan Museum of Art: 15; Courtesy The Board of Trustees, National Gallery of Art, Washington: 29; Lee Stalsworth: 10 (right); courtesy The State Hermitage Museum: 30 (right), 31 (right); courtesy Walker Art Center, Minneapolis: 28 (left); courtesy The Andy Warhol Foundation/CORBIS: 9 (left); courtesy Whitney Museum of American Art: 41 (left)